BENEDICT XVI

BENEDICT XVI
ESSAYS AND REFLECTIONS ON HIS PAPACY

EDITOR, SISTER MARY ANN WALSH, RSM
Director of Media Relations
United States Conference of Catholic Bishops

Greeting from the Vatican
CARDINAL TARCISIO BERTONE
Secretary of State

Foreword
KING ABDULLAH II OF JORDAN

Foreword
PRESIDENT SHIMON PERES OF ISRAEL

Preface
CARDINAL FRANCIS GEORGE, OMI
President, United States Conference of Catholic Bishops

Pope Benedict XVI: First Five Years of His Papacy
JOHN THAVIS
Rome Bureau Chief, Catholic News Service

A SHEED & WARD BOOK
ROWMAN & LITTLEFIELD PUBLISHERS, INC.
Lanham • Boulder • New York • Toronto • Plymouth, UK

Published by Sheed & Ward
An imprint of Rowman & Littlefield Publishers, Inc.
4501 Forbes Boulevard, Suite 200, Lanham, Maryland 20706

Estover Road, Plymouth PL6 7PY, United Kingdom

Distributed by National Book Network

British Library Cataloguing in Publication Information Available

Library of Congress Cataloging-in-Publication Data

Benedict XVI : essays and reflections on his papacy / edited by Mary Ann Walsh.
   p. cm.
 Includes bibliographical references and index.
 ISBN 978-1-58051-234-3 (cloth : alk. paper)
 1. Benedict XVI, Pope, 1927- I. Walsh, Mary Ann, Sister, RSM. II. Title: Benedict 16.
III. Title: Benedict the Sixteenth.
 BX1378.6.B49 2010
 282.092–dc22

                                              2010022153

Printed in Canada

♾™ The paper used in this publication meets the minimum requirements of American National Standard for Information Sciences—Permanence of Paper for Printed Library Materials, ANSI/NISO Z39.48-1992.

Previous: Pope Benedict XVI prays in Germany, with the steeples of the Cathedral of Cologne visible in the background, Aug. 18, 2005.

The Pope kneels to pray before the Holy Sepulchre in Jerusalem, May 15, 2009.

CONTENTS

INTRODUCTIONS

8   Greeting from the Vatican
Cardinal Tarcisio Bertone,
Secretary of State, Vatican City

11   Foreword
King Abdullah II of Jordan

12   Foreword
President Shimon Peres of Israel

15   Preface
Cardinal Francis George, OMI
President, United States
Conference of Catholic Bishops

23   Pope Benedict XVI:
First Five Years of His Papacy
John Thavis

Personal Reflections

33   Archbishop Dennis M. Schnurr
of Cincinnati

PART I: PILGRIM

Essays

36   Unity: A Key Priority

43   Europe: Strength, Struggle

48   China: Catholics Together

53   Finding God in Everyone

58   Message from the Blue Mosque

63   Healing for Christians and Jews

70   On the Road

77   Africa: Reconciliation, Justice and Peace

80   A Continental Mission:
Stand for the Poor

83   With Youth: Ever the Catechist

86   Papal Visit 2008: Christ Our Hope

Personal Reflections

40   Bishop William Skylstad of Spokane

47   Archbishop Robert J. Carlson of St. Louis

55   Archbishop Timothy Broglio
for the Military Services USA

84   Cardinal Francis George, OMI,
Archbishop of Chicago

90   Nancy Wiechec, Visual Media Manager,
Catholic News Service

95   Sister Mary Ann Walsh, RSM,
Director of Media Relations, USCCB

96   Helen Osman, Secretary for
Communications, USCCB

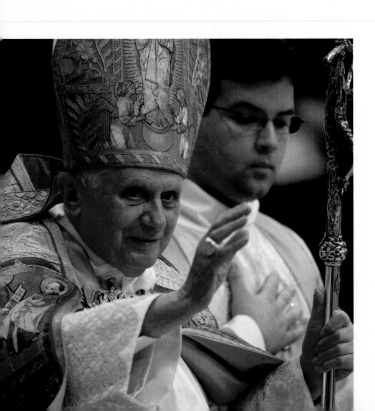

Pope Benedict XVI blesses the crowd in St. Peter's Basilica after creating 23 new cardinals Nov. 24, 2007.

PART II: PASTOR

Essays

100 Giving the Look of Love They Crave

107 Turning to Altötting, Inspired by Mary

108 Arms of the Man

113 The Teachable Garment

119 Music: Joy to His World

123 The Word Has a Face, the Person, Christ

127 Pope Benedict XVI, Model Liturgist

134 Mass Participation from Within

137 Shepherding Cats

142 The Heart of a Disciple

145 *Quaerere Deum*, to Seek God

146 Priesthood Rooted in Prayer

150 Searing Pain of Abuse

Personal Reflections

103 Archbishop Timothy Dolan of New York

117 Archbishop John C. Nienstedt of Saint Paul and Minneapolis

124 Cardinal John Foley, Grand Master of the Order of the Holy Sepulchre of Jerusalem

132 Archbishop George J. Lucas of Omaha

141 Cardinal Edward Egan, Archbishop Emeritus of New York

149 Cardinal Justin Rigali, Archbishop of Philadelphia

153 Cardinal Seán P. O'Malley, Archbishop of Boston

PART III: PROPHET

Essays

156 Caritas in Veritate

161 Ethics and Economics

164 First Justice, Then Charity

167 Human Rights

168 Human Life and Bioethics

171 The Peace Pope

174 Migration: A Sign of the Times

177 Leading the Green Revolution

184 "Friending" Is Evangelizing

187 Family: Basis for Society

188 Faith and Political Life

193 A Challenge to Catholic Educators

194 Hope for Today

Personal Reflections

159 Archbishop Gregory M. Aymond of New Orleans

182 Archbishop Emeritus Joseph A. Fiorenza of Galveston-Houston

RESOURCES

198 The Life and Ministry of Pope Benedict XVI

212 Key Writings of Pope Benedict XVI

214 Contributors

219 Acknowledgments

220 Index

GREETING FROM THE VATICAN

Dear Friends in Christ,

I am pleased to introduce this collection of essays which the United States Conference of Catholic Bishops has issued to mark the first five years of the pontificate of His Holiness Pope Benedict XVI.

As the Successor of Peter, the Pope is the shepherd of the entire flock of Christ (cf. *Jn* 21:15ff.) and the head of the College of Bishops which by the Lord's will has succeeded to the place of the Apostles. Before his election to the papacy, the Holy Father was already known as an outstanding theologian and, as Prefect of the Congregation for the Doctrine of Faith, he had been entrusted with vigilance over the Church's custody of the deposit of faith. In these first years of his pontificate Pope Benedict XVI has brought these rare gifts of knowledge, wisdom and experience to his Petrine ministry of confirming his brothers and sisters in the faith (cf. *Lk* 12:32) and proclaiming the saving truth and beauty of the Gospel to the people of our time.

It is my hope that this book will not only illustrate the program of evangelical witness and fidelity to the Church's living Tradition which has guides these first years of the Holy Father's ministry, but also inspire its readers to take up his invitation to recognize "That faith sheds new light on all things, and that the Gospel reveals the noble vocation and sublime destiny of every man and woman" (*Address at the White House*, Washington, 16 April 2008).

Cardinal Tarcisio Bertone
Secretary of State

Pope Benedict XVI presides over the closing of the Synod of Bishops on
"The Word of God in the Life and Mission of the Church," St. Peter's Basilica, Oct. 26, 2008.

Foreword

BY KING ABDULLAH II OF JORDAN

It is a special honour for me to be asked to contribute a foreword for this book, commemorating the first five years in the papacy of His Holiness Pope Benedict XVI.

In May 2009, my family and I joined dignitaries from across Jordanian society, Muslim and Christian, in welcoming Pope Benedict XVI as he began his first pilgrimage to Jordan and the Holy Land. Rania and I met with His Holiness in 2005 to discuss the vital need for interfaith dialogue. Last year, we, like Jordanians everywhere, were proud to introduce him to Jordan's religious heritage and enduring traditions of tolerance.

Pope Benedict XVI reciprocated our welcome with respect and warm goodwill. Throughout his visit, he spoke with loving encouragement to all, especially young people. His Holiness spoke of his own deep faith, but also of the important common ground between Christianity and Islam—the central commandment of both faiths: to love God and love our fellow human beings.

Pope Benedict XVI's visit will long be remembered in Jordan. But at this critical time in history, its impact goes far beyond. Today, Muslims and Christians make up more than half the world's population. Misunderstanding and conflict between us would devastate all humanity. Working together is essential to the future all of us want: a healthy planet, peace among nations, the end to poverty, and bright futures for today's children. To me, these efforts and more are global expressions of the "love of neighbour" that God commands.

By the bridges he is working to build between faiths, by his engagement in a global dialogue of mutual respect, His Holiness has won tremendous appreciation. His words of wisdom have reached millions of people on every continent. It is my hope that together, we can expand this dialogue to engage all our people in finding their common ground. For Muslims such an endeavour is an integral part of faith. For, God Almighty has said in the Holy Quran: *O humankind! We created you from a male and female, and made you into peoples and tribes that you may know each other.* (49:13)

Nowhere are our shared interests clearer than in the cause of peace between Israel and the Palestinians. "Everything that can be seen in these countries," said His Holiness, "cries out for reconciliation, justice and peace." A special concern is safeguarding the multifaith identity of Jerusalem, Holy City to all three monotheistic faiths—in His Holiness's words, "a microcosm of our globalized world." His call to conscience and his global statesmanship are vitally important to achieving the only settlement that will last—two sovereign, recognized states, with freedom and statehood for Palestinians, and the security and acceptance Israelis need.

These and other challenges of our age call us to come together, on common ground, to do God's will on earth. In this effort, Pope Benedict XVI has raised his voice for reason, justice, and love. May his efforts continue fruitful for many years to come.

King Abdullah II of Jordan and his family prepare to meet with Pope Benedict, May 8, 2009.

King Abdullah of Jordan

FOREWORD

BY PRESIDENT SHIMON PERES OF ISRAEL

From the start, Pope Benedict XVI made it his mission to deepen the religious faith and emphasize its positive meaning. Within his concept, he built bridges of friendship between the Catholic Church and the Jewish people. This is encapsulated in his commonly used greeting of *Shalom, peace be with you* and further reinforced by his uncompromising statement that it was time for Catholics to heal the wounds that for too long have undermined relations between Christians and Jews.

Indeed, his journey of dialogue, reconciliation and understanding was made tangible by his historic pilgrimage to Israel—the Holy Land—in May 2009. Representing the translation of words into actions, intentions into deeds, his visit deeply touched the hearts of the people of Israel. By initiating his visit at the President's residence, Pope Benedict XVI moved my heart profoundly.

Following in the footsteps of Jesus, under the gaze of the Jewish Prophets, while treading on Biblical paths common to both religions—Catholic and Jewish—significantly contributed to realizing the vision of peace and inter-religious dialogue towards which we are striving.

Refusing to rest on his laurels, on January 17 of this year, Pope Benedict XVI created yet another historic milestone in Catholic-Jewish relations when he visited the Great Synagogue of Rome. This represented yet another illustration of his outstretched hand in peace and commitment to his meaningful mission.

We are proud to reach out for his hand and take it, as we pray together for peace. The peoples of the Holy Land yearn for peace, and we pray that the cherished hope shared by the three Abrahamic faiths who love this land equally will be realized. The constructive dialogue struck by the Catholic Church and the Jewish people will serve as an inspiration. Together we shall continue our quest for a better and brighter future for the peoples of this region and the world at large. And it is of the essence that we build it together as a legacy of a better tomorrow for the generations to come.

This book is a distinct message. A message that must be heeded. Pope Benedict's journey is a journey of love, and we are only too happy to join him on this road.

From Jerusalem we shall pray to the Lord of peace and friendship.

Shimon Peres

Pope Benedict shakes hands with
President Shimon Peres at Tel Aviv's
Ben Gurion International Airport, May 11, 2009.

Preface

BY CARDINAL FRANCIS GEORGE, OMI
PRESIDENT, UNITED STATES CONFERENCE OF CATHOLIC BISHOPS

The election of Pope Benedict XVI on April 19, 2005, seems as if it occurred just yesterday. Since that day, we have seen the emergence on the world stage of a man who has captured the hearts not only of Catholics but also of people of many faiths and of none, all across the globe. This book notes the impact of the modest and scholarly Joseph Ratzinger, who has been placed by grace and election before us as Pope Benedict XVI.

Pope Benedict assumed the papacy as a renowned scholar, a prolific writer and an insightful theologian. Such characterizations would not necessarily be seen as qualifications for leadership in a world beset by war between nations and within souls. Yet since that April day of 2005, Pope Benedict has shown himself to be a man for the troubled times that have scarred the beginnings of the 21st century as they marked the duration of the 20th.

Only those who were privileged to know him personally before his election understood that, beyond his great erudition, he carries within him the qualities of a great pope for our times, with a sensitive pastoral heart that would lead him beyond even his prior fields of endeavor.

He was 78 years old when elected, and he advised friends in the College of Cardinals that, unlike his well-traveled predecessor, he wouldn't be a globetrotter. Soon, however, he realized that there is no substitute for going out personally to greet people, to assuage hurt, to preach the Gospel of Christ. He has

Pope Benedict greets a young boy after Mass commemorating the 50th anniversary of the election of Pope John XXIII, Oct. 28, 2008.

already made more than 12 foreign journeys and 18 others within Italy. His first trip was to his native Germany, just four months after his election, to gather with young people at World Youth Day and celebrate their life in Christ. Three years later, in 2008, he traveled thousands of miles to Australia for another World Youth Day.

Pope Benedict recognizes the need to build bridges of friendship and understanding with the Muslim community. In his 2006 trip to Turkey, he visited a mosque and underscored our shared responsibility to defend religious freedom and promote peace. The same themes were on his mind when he visited Israel, Jordan and the Palestinian territories in 2009. Of all his travels, most memorable to me, of course, was his visit to Washington and New York in April 2008. The liturgies at Nationals Park in Washington and at Yankee Stadium and St. Patrick's Cathedral in New York City were moments of deep prayer shared by thousands who attended and by many thousands more via television. His visits to the White House and Ground Zero were moments of national pride, and we Americans sensed he loved our nation as we do.

This warm, pastoral nature that has infused his pontificate has been

Pope Benedict XVI reaches out to Archbishop Daniel E. Pilarczyk at a meeting with U.S. bishops at the Basilica of the National Shrine of the Immaculate Conception in Washington, April 16, 2008.

extended to young and old. In a meeting with First Communicants in Rome just days after his installation, he spoke of the importance of attending Sunday Mass. When one child asked what to do if your parents won't take you to church, Pope Benedict suggested that others, like grandparents, might be willing. The scene, televised by Italian state television, brought smiles of understanding across the nation as the Vicar of Christ set out to help solve a child's problem. He understood.

He proved equally pastoral in dealing with the blight of clergy sexual abuse of young people. He hoped to personally heal people when he met with victims of the crime during his visits to the United States, Australia and most recently Malta. He's promised to meet with others. Those who witnessed his meeting in Washington with men and women who had been victimized by priests saw that those who were hurt could find in him someone to cry with them, to model the vulnerability of Christ. They sensed his own sorrow at their suffering. Holding their hands, he revealed a pastor's care through his human touch.

Long before these meetings, the Pope had studied the records of cases and taken decisive steps to address both the bureaucratic slowness that exacerbates wounds and the culture of entitlement that allows such crimes to occur.

He faces the challenge of encouraging the many thousands of priests who are betrayed by the sin of their brothers and of speaking to the millions of Catholics horrified that such offenses occurred in the Church they love.

The Pope brought a pastoral kindness to global affairs when he was among the first world leaders to congratulate Barack Obama after his election as the first African American president of the United States. The usual protocol was to wait until the inauguration to send congratulations, but the Pope felt that the election of a president who is also the first African American to hold this office warranted an immediate communiqué.

His pastoral nature shows in other ways. The Pope chose his name after Pope Benedict XV, who sought to be a peacemaker during World War I. Given Pope Benedict XVI's own youth in war-torn Germany, the horrors of war evoke deep sorrow and compassion in him. As pope he has spoken out passionately as nation threatens nation, especially in the Middle East. He stood for peace when he visited Jerusalem, home of the Christian, Jewish and Islamic communities. He worked for peace when he stood at holy sites like the Blue Mosque in Istanbul, where he reflected beside Muslim leaders, and at Israel's Western Wall, where he left a personal prayer between stones.

Pope Benedict XVI meets with cardinals from around the world in the Synod Hall at the Vatican, Nov. 23, 2007.

The Pope works at a summer residence in Les Combes, Valle d'Aosta, July 11, 2006.

The Pope's mission is to unify people. He cares not only for world solidarity but also for inner harmony or communion within the Church. He has sought to make peace with those who have formally left the Church through schism, such as the followers of the late Archbishop Marcel Lefebvre. He receives representatives of the other Christian churches and ecclesial communities to advance the cause of unity within the body of Christ.

This pastoral sense shows as well in his three encyclicals. The first, *God Is Love* (*Deus Caritas Est*), was a simple yet profound explanation of love as self-giving. He spoke practically when he wrote about sexual love, and he stressed that sexual expression must be marked by "concern and care for the other" (no. 6).

His second, *On Christian Hope* (*Spe Salvi*), emphasized God's personal nature and the hope that comes from a relationship with God, a hope that can sustain individuals through any trial.

The third encyclical, *Charity in Truth* (*Caritas in Veritate*), explained how ethical values must guide everyone: from Wall Street traders and financiers who affect global markets, to policy makers who allow a minority of the people in the world to use the vast majority of the world's natural resources. The Pope noted the importance of individual human beings: *"the primary capital to be safeguarded and val-*

ued is man, the human person in his or her integrity" (no. 25). He was to-the-point when he said that the right to food and water is universal and part of the basic right to life of all human beings, without distinction or discrimination.

More than five years ago, prayers from around the world and within the Sistine Chapel asked the Holy Spirit to guide the College of Cardinals in electing the Bishop of Rome. The electors sought the right man for the right time for the Church and the world. As Pope Benedict XVI pastors the Church, there is comfort in knowing that the Holy Spirit, through this pope's ministry, continues to guide and inspire the people of God. ∎

In this sense it is true that anyone who does not know God, even though he may entertain all kinds of hopes, is ultimately without hope, without the great hope that sustains the whole of life (cf. Eph 2:12). Man's great, true hope which holds firm in spite of all disappointments can only be God—God who has loved us and who continues to love us "to the end," until all "is accomplished."

—On Christian Hope (Spe Salvi)*, no. 27*

Pope Benedict looks from a plane over Vatican City, Sept. 21, 2005.

POPE BENEDICT XVI: FIRST FIVE YEARS OF HIS PAPACY

BY JOHN THAVIS

ROME BUREAU CHIEF, CATHOLIC NEWS SERVICE

At his inaugural Mass in April 2005, Pope Benedict XVI said his primary mission was to help lead people out of the modern "desert" of empty values, alienation and injustice and toward the light of Christ.

During his first five years in office, the German pontiff has never lost that critical focus.

Whether addressing the United Nations or grade-school children, in off-the-cuff remarks at his general audiences or in the carefully reasoned arguments of his three encyclicals, Benedict has returned again and again to his number-one agenda item: the human person and his or her relationship with truth, love and God.

For the Pope, this is not just a theoretical exercise. As he said in his encyclical *Charity in Truth* (*Caritas in Veritate*), the root causes of the current economic crisis and so many social injustices in the modern world are "ideo-

logical rejection of God and an atheism of indifference" (no. 78).

Without God as a reference point, he has argued, erosion of fundamental values is inevitable.

"Human life is a relationship . . . and the basic relationship is with the Creator," he told Rome priests in March 2006. "A world emptied of God, a world that has forgotten God, loses life and falls into a culture of death."

One has to appreciate this line of attack in order to understand Pope Benedict's papal ministry so far.

Elected on the conclave's second day, April 19, 2005, he has turned expectations upside down: instead of staying home, Benedict has traveled to every continent; instead of curbing dialogue with non-Christians, he has taken it to a new, more urgent level; and instead of reigning as a doctrinaire disciplinarian, he has approached his audiences as a teacher.

---

 eter's current successor takes on as his primary task the duty to work tirelessly to rebuild the full and visible unity of all Christ's followers. This is his ambition, his impelling duty. He is aware that good intentions do not suffice for this. Concrete gestures that enter hearts and stir consciences are essential, inspiring in everyone that inner conversion that is the prerequisite for all ecumenical progress.

—Address to cardinals on the day after the Pope's election, April 20, 2005

As universal pastor, the Pope has led Catholics back to the roots of their faith. In books, sermons and papal documents, he has catechized the faithful on Christianity's foundational practices and beliefs, ranging from the *Confessions of St. Augustine* to the Sign of the Cross.

This "back to basics" approach is reflected in his first encyclical, *God Is Love* (*Deus Caritas Est*), and his book *Jesus of Nazareth*. Both texts insist on the vital connection between the Gospel of Christ and sacrificial love and charitable works. His message to the Church and the world—sounding a little strange coming from one of the world's most erudite theologians—was that Christian faith really is that simple.

As he said during Mass in a packed St. Patrick's Cathedral in New York in 2008, Christianity is not a set of rules.

"Perhaps we have lost sight of this: in a society where the Church seems legalistic and 'institutional' to many people, our most urgent challenge is to communicate the joy born of faith and the experience of God's love," he said.

The Pope has tried to keep this positive, thoughtful message in the forefront—not always easy in a culture dominated by entertainment, controversy and superficiality. One topic that has resonated with the media and his listeners is ecology. By approving a host of environmentally friendly projects, including the installation of solar panels on a Vatican roof, Pope Benedict has won a reputation as the "green pope." For him, of course, it's a natural "God issue": he consistently reminds us that the Church's teaching on environmental protection flows directly from an awareness of a divine Creator.

The human relationship with God is also central to Pope Benedict's dialogue with non-Christian religions.

Guards in traditional fezzes lead the Holy Father through the streets of Jerusalem, May 15, 2009.

Pope Benedict meets with the grand mufti of Jerusalem at the Dome of the Rock in Jerusalem, May 12, 2009.

✠ With Muslims in particular, he has emphasized the connection between faith and reason and insisted that violence in the name of religion is an affront to God. At the same time, he has warned the West that unless its secularized society rediscovers religious values, it cannot hope to engage in real dialogue with Islamic and other religious cultures.

These were two primary themes of the Pope's 2006 speech in Regensburg, Germany. The speech prompted widespread criticism among Muslims for quoting a medieval scholar who said Islam had spread its religion "by the sword." The Pope, clearly surprised by the reaction, moved quickly to resolve the issue, saying those words did not reflect his own thoughts and apologizing for the misunderstanding.

In retrospect, Vatican officials say Regensburg opened a new chapter in the Vatican's 40-year dialogue with the Muslim world. A summit with Muslim leaders was quickly arranged, and a high-level Vatican-Muslim forum was established. When the Pope traveled to Turkey in late 2006, he stunned even some top aides when he stood and prayed next to a Muslim cleric in Istanbul's Blue Mosque. This powerful but simple gesture of prayer showed his deep respect for Muslim believers and put Regensburg behind him.

Pope Benedict has not had an easy ride with the world's media. His talks about the compelling case for faith rarely make headlines, and despite Vatican efforts to promote him on YouTube and other new media, no one really thinks this pope's message can be reduced to sound bites or tweets.

In 2008, his lifting of the excommunications of four traditionalist bishops stirred up a media storm when it turned out that one of the four, Bishop Richard Williamson, had recently given an interview minimizing Jewish suffering under the Nazi regime. Suddenly, it seemed that the Pope was rehabilitating a Holocaust denier.

To correct this impression, the Vatican worked with its usual deliberate speed—but it soon became apparent that in the world of instant communications, that wasn't fast enough. In the end, the Pope drew a hard line on the renegade bishop's opinions on the Holocaust and strongly reiterated the Church's teachings against anti-Semitism. It satisfied Jewish dialogue partners but left many people wondering why it wasn't said earlier.

Perhaps the most surprising aspect of the episode was the Pope's remarkably personal letter to the world's bishops two months later. He wrote that he was saddened at the willingness of some Catholics to believe he was changing direction on Catholic-Jewish relations and their readiness to "attack me with open hostility." It was a rare glimpse into the emotional sensitivity of the German pope, who usually gives the impression of being imperturbable.

If the Bishop Williamson affair marked a low point in media relations for Pope Benedict, his 2008 trip to the United States was a high point. One reason was that he addressed the clerical sex abuse issue early and head-on. He told reporters on his plane from Rome that when he read the victims' case histories, he could not imagine how a priest could betray his mission to be an agent of God's love.

"We are deeply ashamed and will do all possible that this cannot happen in the future," he said. These unusually direct remarks were followed by the Pope's unscheduled meeting in Washington with five sex abuse victims, a moving and tearful encounter.

The Pope's six days in the United States brought his own identity into clearer focus for Americans. He set forth a moral challenge on issues ranging from economic justice to abortion, but without coming across as doctrinaire or bullying. At a Mass with 45,000 people in Washington, he said U.S. society was at a crossroads.

"We see clear signs of a disturbing breakdown in the very foundations of society: signs of alienation, anger and polarization on the part of many of our contemporaries; increased violence; a weakening of the moral sense; a coars-

Priests and seminarians rush to greet Pope Benedict XVI after his Mass at Yankee Stadium in New York, April 20, 2008.

ening of social relations; and a growing ✠ people, he brought this argument
forgetfulness of God," he said. home by talking about environmental
degradation: "The earth itself groans
Yet the Pope's challenge was under the weight of consumerist greed
framed in terms of appreciation for and irresponsible exploitation."
America's traditional blend of religion
and morality, and he punctuated his Pope Benedict met three times
message with quotations from George with then President George W. Bush,
Washington and Franklin Roosevelt. and they found wide areas of agreement
He warned that the country's secular- on pro-life and family issues. The Pope's
moral balance was on the verge of tip- first meeting with President Barack
ping toward a godless, individualistic Obama, at the Vatican in 2009, was also
form of freedom. Addressing young cordial and upbeat—surprising some

U.S. Catholics who have criticized ✠ Obama on pro-life issues. But that, too, is Benedict's style: moral prodding, not blasting. In a typically understated way, he handed Obama a copy of the Vatican's 2008 document on biomedical ethics, *The Dignity of a Person* (*Dignitas Personae*), prompting the president to quip, "I will have some reading to do on the plane."

As head of the Church, Pope Benedict has focused on the fundamentals. When he convened the Synod of Bishops in 2008, he chose as its theme not any of the hot-button issues like priestly celibacy or the role of women and laypeople, but the Bible in the life of the Church. He proclaimed a special Year of St. Paul to rekindle missionary awareness among Catholics and followed it with a Year for Priests to highlight what he described as a vital ministry in trying times.

His emphasis on prayer and quiet contemplation came through at his first World Youth Day vigil in Cologne, Germany, in 2005. As hundreds of thousands of young people chanted his name, Pope Benedict remained silent and put his finger to his lips. Such moments made it clear that he would not try to imitate his predecessor's often playful encounters with younger audiences, with foot tapping, arm waving and jokes. Instead, he led them in adoration of the Eucharist.

The young people recognized the shift in tone and respected it.

"We saw John Paul II a lot on camera. He was charismatic and would give you a hug. This pope has another way of being close to you and showing his interest in you," remarked Veronique Rondeau, a Montreal student who said Pope Benedict had asked questions and listened intently during lunch with a group of youth.

Although he approved wider use of the older Tridentine Mass— applauded by Catholic traditionalists—the Pope's own liturgies at the Vatican follow the modern rite. Close observers have noticed a few significant changes, however—a cross at the center of the altar, traditional vestments and the insistence that those taking Communion from the Pope kneel and receive the host on the tongue.

Benedict has kept a shepherd's watch over minority Christian communities worldwide, insisting publicly and privately on legal protection of religious rights. Through diplomatic representatives, he has pressed governments in places like India and Pakistan, where Christians have been targeted and killed. As he declared to the United Nations in 2008: "It is inconceivable that believers should have to suppress a part of themselves—their faith—in order to be active citizens."

Pope Benedict stands on Mount Nebo in Jordan, where it is said Moses was given a view of the Promised Land, May 9, 2009.

The Pope also laid the groundwork for the Church's revitalization in China, which is viewed as a primary missionary zone of the future. In contrast with the Roman Curia's traditionally discreet and behind-the-scenes efforts to prod the Chinese government, Pope Benedict brought it all into the open. His 55-page letter to Chinese Catholics in 2007 strongly criticized the government's limits on the Church's

✠ activities, invited civil authorities to a fresh and serious dialogue, and set guidelines to favor cooperation between clandestine Catholic communities and those officially registered with the government.

Benedict's style is sometimes described as academic. But as a skilled teacher, he's also found creative images and language to bring the power of the faith home to his listeners—on one occasion, comparing the transforming impact of the Eucharist to nuclear fission, "an intimate explosion of good conquering evil" (World Youth Day, 2005).

A year after his election, the Pope hosted 40,000 youths one evening in St. Peter's Square. Their faces lit by the evening sun, the young people listened raptly as the pontiff quietly answered their questions about his own youth. He described how the brutality of the Nazi regime led him to become a priest. He acknowledged self-doubts about whether he could be celibate his whole life. He said he wondered whether he had the interpersonal skills to be a good pastor. It was a defining moment of Pope Benedict's young pontificate: he understood that simple personal experiences, no less than theological arguments, have the power to inspire. ■

Above: Pope Benedict greets pilgrims in St. Peter's Square, Oct. 17, 2007.

Opposite: Pope Benedict XVI blesses a girl as the eucharistic gifts are presented at the Mass at Nationals Park, Washington, April 17, 2008.

PHOTO BY POPE BENEDICT XVI

ARCHBISHOP DENNIS M. SCHNURR • ARCHBISHOP OF CINCINNATI

DURING MY YEARS as general secretary of the United States Conference of Catholic Bishops, I would frequently travel to Rome, and oftentimes I would see Cardinal Ratzinger making his daily trek across St. Peter's Square from his apartment to his office. He would mingle with the people in the square while garbed in a simple black cassock. There was no indication that he was a cardinal, much less prefect of the Congregation for the Doctrine of the Faith. Often he was drafted by a group to serve as its photographer. This he did willingly and with a generous smile. As far as the group members were concerned, they had just been assisted by one of the local priests—and Cardinal Ratzinger was quite content to leave them with that understanding. I often wonder today if any of those tourists know their photographer moved on to become Pope Benedict XVI.

PART I ILGRIM

Unity: A Key Priority

BY FATHER RONALD ROBERSON, CSP

The day after his election, Pope Benedict XVI called the cardinals together in the Sistine Chapel to outline his vision of the papacy. He told them that the fostering of the unity of Christians would lie at the pinnacle of his ministry.

For Pope Benedict, the central role of the Bishop of Rome is to be the guarantor of the unity of the followers of Christ, through which all the local churches are in full communion with one another and Christ himself. Pope Benedict would repeat this conviction in a letter to the Catholic bishops on March 10, 2009, regarding the remission of the excommunication of four bishops of the Society of St. Pius X. Here the Pope wrote that ecumenism—the promotion of Christian unity—is part of the "supreme and fundamental priority of the Church and of the Successor of Peter at the present time."

The Pope has encouraged the continuation of ecumenical contacts and dialogues that began under his prede-cessors. Among his first trips outside Italy was a visit to Istanbul, Turkey, in November 2006. There he met with Patriarch Bartholomew of Constantinople and signed with him a Common Declaration in which the two church leaders expressed the joy they felt as brothers and renewed their commitment to move towards full communion.

Pope Benedict has also encouraged deeper cooperation with the Anglican Communion and other communities that trace their roots back to the Reformation. In November 2006, he received Archbishop Rowan Williams of Canterbury during his visit to Rome and signed a Common Declaration with him in which they praised the "significant elements of shared faith" that have been discovered in the theological dialogue between the two churches and the "practical cooperation and service."

Due in part to his German origins, the Pope also has a special interest in the dialogue with the Lutherans. In a message addressed to the Lutheran World Federation for its 60th anniversary in

Pope Benedict XVI greets Bernice A. King, daughter of Rev. Dr. Martin Luther King Jr., during his 2008 visit to the United States.

Previous: Pope Benedict looks out from a balcony of the papal residence, Aug. 12, 2007.

March 2007, the Pope praised the "always fruitful" dialogue between Lutherans and Catholics and the great progress that has been made in relations since the Second Vatican Council. He called these improved relations a "gift of the Holy Spirit," which urges both sides "not to slacken in our ecumenical endeavors."

The Pope has also introduced a note of realism in the Catholic Church's ecumenical efforts. He has reaffirmed the teaching of Vatican II that, while the fullness of the one Church of Christ is found in the Catholic Church, there are also authentic and salvific elements of the Church that exist in other communions. He has also pointed out that the evolving teaching of some churches of the West on moral matters, especially pertaining to sexuality, present new barriers on the path towards full communion.

But there can be no doubt that Pope Benedict XVI is firmly committed to the restoration of the unity of the followers of Jesus. He knows how deeply division compromises the Christian proclamation of the Gospel, and how much stronger it would be if all Christians spoke with one voice. He is making every effort to hasten the day when the world will see Christians fully united. ∎

Pope Benedict walks with the Ecumenical Patriarch Bartholomew I during the papal visit to Turkey, Nov. 29-30, 2006.

FRUITFUL DIALOGUE

BISHOP WILLIAM SKYLSTAD • BISHOP OF SPOKANE

PERHAPS ONE OF MY most memorable visits with Cardinal Joseph Ratzinger before he became our Holy Father was the group meeting of Region XII bishops with him during our *ad limina* visit in 2004. Since our region is relatively small, the entire group was readily able to engage the cardinal. We were scheduled to meet for what we thought would be about an hour; but as it turned out, the meeting went over two hours. The bishops were amazed at his pastoral sensitivities and the ease of a very fruitful conversation. We still talk about that meeting several years later.

Pope Benedict addresses Jewish leaders at Park East Synagogue in New York City, April 18, 2008.

Opposite: The Pope greets Venerable Dr. Jongmae Kenneth Park of the Korean Buddhist Taego Order at the Pope John Paul II Cultural Center in Washington, April 17, 2008.

Europe:
Strength, Struggle

BY FATHER ANDREW SMALL, OMI

Key to understanding Pope Benedict XVI's life and ministry is knowing his complex relationship with his European heritage. Both its roots and troubles are part of him. He was raised in the staunchly Catholic Bavarian part of Germany, surrounded by visible and comforting expressions of his homeland's Catholic heritage.

Discomfiting, however, was the upheaval he witnessed in a Europe beset by two world wars, the second of which briefly swept up the young Joseph Ratzinger. The wars caused deep divisions in Europe that went beyond political life. In that context, Pope John XXIII convoked the Second Vatican Council, and Father Ratzinger attended as a theological adviser to the German bishops. There he saw firsthand another kind of upheaval, this time within the Church. Eventually he began to question the so-called "spirit of the Council," that came to justify changes in church life, preferring to emphasize continuity rather than rupture with the past.

In this climate, Europe experienced a dramatic decline in church membership and attendance. Worse still, Europe's Christian heritage slowly eroded from the public square as churches emptied to become historical sites rather than places of worship. This has been a constant concern to Pope Benedict.

In 2004, Cardinal Ratzinger had leveled a pointed critique at the draft constitution of the European Union for eliminating any reference to the importance of Europe's

The Pope visits the concentration camp at Auschwitz, May 28, 2006.

Pilgrims hold a sign greeting the Holy Father at World Youth Day in Cologne, Germany. The Pope joined the festival on Aug. 18, staying until Aug. 21.

Christian roots. For him, history and culture combined to form a people. Through the draft's failure to recognize the religious roots of European culture, the fabric of European society and the possibility for genuine progress was being undermined.

In 2006, he explained his concerns to members of the European People's Party and warned against the "secular intransigence" prevalent in European society that displays "immaturity" in refusing to dialogue with Europe's religious tradition. Such intransigence jeopardizes the dignity of the person in two ways, he said. First, "life in all its stages, from the first moment of conception to natural death" is threatened; the "right of parents to educate their children" is weakened,

and the "natural structure of the family as a union between a man and a woman based on marriage" is not afforded its "irreplaceable social role."

Second, he said, religious freedom is undermined when the Church's right to raise concerns about social developments and to educate consciences about such issues is itself proscribed or seen as a form of discrimination by civil laws. The Pope affirmed that when the Church intervenes in public debate, expressing reservations or recalling various principles, "this does not constitute a form of intolerance or an interference, since such interventions are aimed solely at enlightening consciences, enabling them to act freely and responsibly, according to the true demands of justice, even when this should conflict with situations of power and personal interest."

Pope Benedict has repeated this concern, calling the abandonment of Europe's religious heritage by its elected leaders quite simply "apostasy." In a visit to the Czech Republic in September 2009, Benedict reaffirmed the "irreplaceable role of Christianity for the formation of the conscience of each generation" of Europeans. The Church's posture is to fight not for its own existence, but for the "basic truths" of the human person, without which the identity of Europe itself is undermined, he said. ■

Opposite: Pope Benedict XVI arrives for a youth rally at St. Joseph's Seminary in Yonkers, N.Y., April 19, 2008.

Bringing Him a Piece of Home

ARCHBISHOP ROBERT J. CARLSON • ARCHBISHOP OF ST. LOUIS

I HAVE HAD the privilege of meeting His Holiness Pope Benedict XVI on three different occasions—at the Pallium Mass in 2009, a general audience in October 2008, and a private meeting in the spring of 2006. It was then that I had just finished a pilgrimage from Germany to Poland, and among the places visited was the birthplace of Pope Benedict XVI in Marktl Am Inn, Germany. Stopping in Rome on the way back to the United States, I had the opportunity to meet with the Holy Father; but, because the meeting was not planned, I had nothing to give him. Looking through my luggage, I noticed a small booklet, bearing an official stamp, from the parish where he was baptized. It was immediately obvious he was not familiar with some of the pictures, and a tender moment occurred as his eyes captured that precious time in his life. It is that same joy and tenderness that he shares with you each time he meets you in crowds large and small.

The Pope greets the UN assembly in New York, April 18, 2008.

Opposite: An African child receives the Pope's blessing at Mass in Yaoundé, Cameroon, March 19, 2009.

CHINA: CATHOLICS TOGETHER

BY VIRGINIA FARRIS

ope Benedict XVI listened raptly to Mozart's *Requiem* Mass in D Minor. But this May 2008 concert was unique; it was performed by the China Philharmonic Orchestra and the Shanghai Opera House Chorus. In thanking the performers, the Pope said he wanted "to reach out to your entire people, with a special thought for those of your fellow citizens who share faith in Jesus and are united through a particular spiritual bond with the Successor of Peter."

Early in his pontificate, the Pope demonstrated his desire to improve relations with China. He sent an official Vatican delegation to Beijing in June 2006 and convened a special Commission for the Catholic Church in China. He also directed that the Vatican's Web site include a Chinese version.

In June 2007, Pope Benedict issued a historic letter to the Catholic Church in China. In it, he expressed hope for a dialogue with the People's Republic of China so that they could "work together for the good of the Chinese people and for peace in the world." But he devoted most of the letter to solidarity with the suffering of Chinese Catholics and affirmed that the Church in China is part of the "one, holy, catholic, and apostolic" Church.

This call to unity means two things. First, the Pope wants the Church in China to be in communion with the Successor of Peter. In contrast, the government wants obedience from the Church. China controls religious activity of the Catholic Church through the Chinese Catholic Patriotic Association (CCPA), which sanctions where people worship and who is ordained bishop, and which insists that church communities registered with it be independent of Rome. Those who have refused to register with the government instead worship in "underground" church communities.

The call to unity also highlights the conflict between "official" and "underground" church communities, a conflict that often centers on the appointment of bishops. The Pope invites all Chinese bishops to be in

The Pope shakes hands with musicians at a concert for the fourth anniversary of his election, April 30, 2009.

communion with him. Some, ordained originally by the "official" Chinese church, have then sought full communion with the Pope and been welcomed. Recently several bishops were ordained with the agreement of both the Vatican and Chinese authorities.

In a May 2009 document highlighting major points of his 2007 letter to Chinese Catholics, Pope Benedict held open the door to negotiations with the People's Republic of China on normalization of relations, but more importantly, he expressed his fraternal closeness to Chinese Catholics as they are in his heart and daily prayer. ∎

Above: Pope Benedict poses for a photo with the Vatican Diplomatic Corps, Aug. 1, 2009.

Opposite: The Pope walks on the grounds at Castel Gandolfo, May 5, 2005.

Saman Hussain presents a gift to Pope Benedict XVI during an interfaith gathering at the Pope John Paul II Cultural Center in Washington, April 17, 2008. The book contains poetic verses from the Qur'an, the sacred book of Islam. The verse presented to the Pope emphasizes the encounter with God as light.

FINDING GOD IN EVERYONE

BY FATHER JAMES MASSA

here will be no peace among the nations without peace among the religions. There will be no peace among the religions without dialogue among the religions," according to Hans Küng, the former university colleague and, at times, theological adversary of Pope Benedict XVI (Speech at Santa Clara University, March 31, 2005). Father Küng and the Pope have been friends since they were young professors at the University of Tübingen in Germany (1966-1969), despite the fact that the two theologians have locked horns on matters of doctrine and practice. The two met at the Pope's summer residence, Castel Gandolfo, shortly after Pope Benedict was elected in 2005, and they are reported to have spoken about interreligious dialogue as the key to building bridges of peace.

Pope Benedict understands that dialogue belongs at the heart of the Church's mission. God has entered into dialogue with human beings by sending his Son, the eternal Word. Faith in Jesus Christ is man's response to God, but it is also a human act that can only be given in dialogue with other believers. The Church, made up of those who have heard the Gospel, wants to communicate God's love and truth to all of humanity, and this can only be done by means of dialogue with the great cultures and religions of humankind.

When the Holy Father visited Washington in April 2008, he met with representatives of five of the great world religions: Judaism, Islam, Hinduism, Buddhism and Jainism. He commended the joint initiatives in charitable works that bring the followers of these and other religions together to ease human suffering and advance public welfare. But Pope Benedict also recognized the broader purpose of interreligious dialogue, which is to discover the truth about humankind's origin and destiny and thereby affirm human dignity. "Only by addressing deeper questions," the Pope said, can the religions "build a solid basis for the peace and security of the human family."

The Pope has reached out to Muslims, who share with Christians a strained history. Despite some rancorous moments, over time scholars from various Islamic schools have responded positively to the Pope's invitation to a dialogue of reason in which religious freedom is prized as a safeguard for the rights of conscience.

In 2006, Pope Benedict visited the Blue Mosque in Istanbul, where he and Istanbul's chief Islamic cleric, Imam Mustafa Cagrici, prayed silently before the *mihrab*, a special niche in a mosque wall, facing Mecca. "Let us pray for brotherhood and the good of humanity!" the Pope said to his host. Out of respect for crucial differences in belief, the Pope advocates multi-religious prayer, which affords the chance to witness to those of differing beliefs and to honor their spiritual practices. ■

Above: The shoeless Pope meets with the grand mufti of Jerusalem and other Muslim leaders at the Dome of the Rock on Temple Mount in Jerusalem, May 12, 2009.

Opposite: Pope Benedict XVI leads his general audience in St. Peter's Square at the Vatican, Nov. 21, 2007.

Following: Pope Benedict XVI and Patriarch Bartholomew I sign a common declaration in Istanbul, Nov. 30, 2006.

Like Meeting an Old Friend

ARCHBISHOP TIMOTHY BROGLIO • ARCHBISHOP FOR THE MILITARY SERVICES

EVEN THOUGH I had met the Holy Father several times in the years that he was a cardinal, I was still apprehensive as I approached him after the general audience in St. Peter's Square some two months after his election to the Chair of Peter. Before I could speak, a warm smile appeared on his face as he took my right hand in both of his and said, "*Ci conosciamo* (we know each other)." He then began to recall my years of service at the Secretariat of State, which he identified by gesturing with his head to indicate the Apostolic Palace. Immediately, he had put me at ease. It was as if I were talking with an old friend.

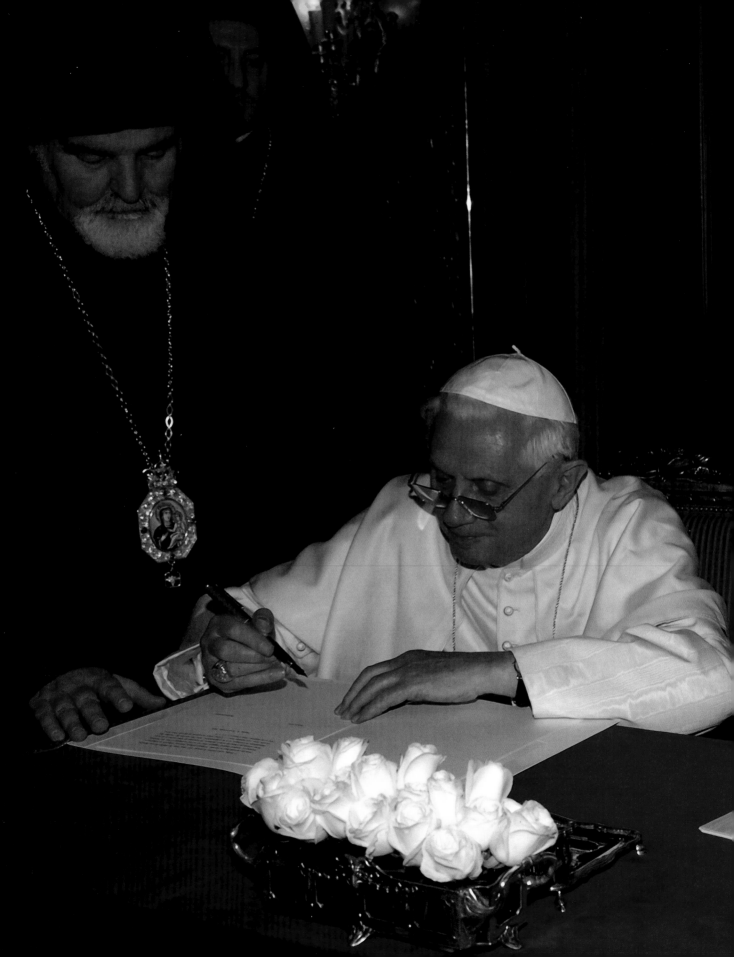

MESSAGE FROM
THE BLUE MOSQUE

BY CINDY WOODEN

When Pope Benedict XVI stood in silent meditation in Istanbul's Blue Mosque, the world took notice.

The fact that the Pope had taken off his shoes and was standing with his arms folded in the same manner as the imam praying next to him was read by many Muslims as a sign of deep respect.

That picture-perfect moment occurred in November 2006, just two months after Pope Benedict had offended many Muslims during a speech on the importance of allowing faith to be informed by reason. In that speech at the University of Regensburg, Germany, the Pope had quoted a medieval Byzantine emperor who said the prophet Mohammed had brought "things only evil and inhuman, such as his command to spread by the sword the faith." The Pope afterward clarified that he was not endorsing the emperor's words, and he expressed regret that Muslims were hurt by the remarks.

In reaction, 138 Muslim scholars from around the world launched an initiative called "A Common Word," writing to Pope Benedict and other Christian leaders to ask for a serious dialogue about values Christians and Muslims hold in common: the obligation to love God and to love one another. The Pope's response was to invite representatives to the Vatican.

The meeting led to the establishment of a new Catholic-Muslim Forum for dialogue, which held its inaugural meeting at the Vatican in November 2008. Professing faith in one God, the Creator of all humanity, obliges Catholics and Muslims to respect one another and to work together to defend human rights and help those who are suffering, Pope Benedict told the 28 Catholic and 28 Muslim participants. The commandments of love of God and love of neighbor are at "the heart of Islam and Christianity alike" and always go together, he said.

Pope Benedict's May 2008 trip to the Holy Land brought further rapprochement with Muslim leaders. The Pope visited a mosque in Jordan,

Pope Benedict XVI and Mustafa Cagrici, the grand mufti of Istanbul, pray in the Blue Mosque in Istanbul, Turkey, Nov. 30, 2006. The historic visit marked the second time a pope has entered a mosque.

made a major address to Muslim scholars there and visited the Dome of the Rock, one of Islam's holiest sites, when he traveled on to Jerusalem.

While the Pope's Muslim hosts mentioned the Regensburg speech, the warm and candid exchanges between the Pope and his Muslim hosts in the Holy Land seemed to signal real progress in relations between Pope Benedict and Muslim leaders and a commitment by both to strengthening cooperation and mutual understanding.

"All believers . . . must leave behind their prejudices and desires for domination, and practice together the basic commandment: to love God with all one's being and love one another as oneself," the Pope said. "It is this that Christians, Jews and Muslims are called to witness in order to honor with facts the God they pray to with their lips." ■

Pope Benedict XVI walks with Muslim clerics as he visits the Blue Mosque in Istanbul.

Opposite: Pope Benedict XVI and Mustafa Cagrici pray in the Blue Mosque.

HEALING FOR CHRISTIANS AND JEWS

BY FATHER JAMES MASSA

An hour or so before sunset on April 18, 2008, an elderly German priest visited the Park East Synagogue in Manhattan to offer Passover greetings to the Jewish community, which was about to begin its Sabbath observance. The cleric was greeted by a choir of children who had donned white yarmulkes similar to the one that he always wears as part of his official uniform. The children sang the "*Shema Yisrael*," the opening words of the Jewish morning and evening prayer: "Hear, O Israel, the LORD is our God. The LORD is one."

Then Rabbi Arthur Schneier officially welcomed the world's most famous priest and noted that he was the first pope ever to visit a Jewish house of worship in the United States. Pope Benedict XVI responded with the greeting that he uses to begin every Mass: Shalom!—*Peace be with you.* Alluding to the Jewish roots of his own faith, he then offered a personal reflection: "I find it moving to recall that Jesus, as a young boy, heard the words of Scripture and prayed in a place such as this. . . ."

From the beginning of his pontificate, Pope Benedict has sought to build bridges of friendship between the Church and the Jewish people. In this work of reconciliation, he follows the path of his predecessor—one set by the Second Vatican Council (1962-1965), which condemned anti-Semitism and declared that God's covenant with the Jews is living and holy.

During the World Youth Day festivities in 2005, Pope Benedict visited the Cologne Synagogue, where he recalled history's most appalling case of anti-Semitism, the Holocaust, or *Shoah*, in which millions of innocent Jews were murdered by the Nazis. As a teenager forced into the German army, he experienced firsthand the "insane racist ideology" that aimed at destroying even Christianity by cutting it off at its Jewish root. The *Shoah* was a time "when the holiness of God was no longer recognized" and

In Jerusalem, the Pope stands near the eternal flame in the
Hall of Remembrance at the Yad Vashem Holocaust Memorial, May 11, 2009.

"contempt was shown for the sacredness of human life," he said. No member of the Church can ever deny or minimize the evil that took place in those years.

In Pope Benedict's view, Catholics have a duty "to heal the wounds that for too long have sullied relations between Christians and Jews." Work for Jewish relations is unique among the Church's interreligious engagements, for "the faith witnessed to by the Jewish Bible is not merely another religion to us, but is the foundation of our own faith."

The Pope believes in vigorous dialogue that does not skirt differences, but that also identifies shared convictions and hopes. He revised the Good Friday Prayer for the Jews in the 1962 Latin Missal by removing offensive imagery and in order to express the hope, based on St. Paul, that by the end of time the Church and the Jewish people would share together in the final blessings of God's Kingdom.

In his bestseller *Jesus of Nazareth*, the Pope entertains a question frequently posed by skeptics: What has Jesus brought to the world, if he has not brought peace and universal prosperity? Pope Benedict XVI answers emphatically by saying that Jesus has brought *God* to the world—the God of Israel! The promises of salvation come to the nations through the preaching of the Gospel of Christ, but their origins lie with the Chosen People of the first covenant, whom God has never stopped loving. ∎

May the names of these victims never perish! May their suffering never be denied, belittled or forgotten! And may all people of good will remain vigilant in rooting out from the heart of man anything that could lead to tragedies such as this! As we stand here in silence, their cry still echoes in our hearts. It is a cry raised against every act of injustice and violence. It is a perpetual reproach against the spilling of innocent blood. It is the cry of Abel rising from the earth to the Almighty.

—Speech at Yad Vashem Holocaust Memorial, May 11, 2009

Previous: The Pope stands at the Western Wall in the Old City of Jerusalem, May 12, 2009.

Opposite: The Pope meets with Rabbi Shear-Yashuv Cohen, the chief rabbi of Haifa, in the Vatican, March 12, 2009.

Following: Pope Benedict XVI attends a ceremony in the Hall of Remembrance at Yad Vashem Holocaust Memorial in Jerusalem, May 11, 2009.

ON THE ROAD

BY JOHN THAVIS

e was supposed to be the "stay-at-home" pope. But his first years in office saw Pope Benedict XVI trekking across the globe: five continents, 14 countries, 60,000 miles.

Just after his 2005 election, the Pope advised us not to expect him to match Pope John Paul II's globe-trotting pace. Days later, he scheduled a trip to World Youth Day in Germany, and the papal odometer began rolling.

As one of the reporters on the papal plane, I've watched Pope Benedict develop his own traveling style. For someone in his 80s, he has remarkable endurance: on his Holy Land pilgrimage in 2009, he presided over 27 major events. At the end of that trip, he strolled to the journalists' section of his plane and offered an analysis of the trip, amazing the weary press.

In country after country, Pope Benedict has surprised his audiences in other ways. Many were expecting the Grand Inquisitor. Instead, the Pope has presented his main message—the importance of faith in God and the hope offered by Christ—in a gently prodding manner that recognizes modern doubts.

In his travels, Pope Benedict relies less on mega-events and more on reasoned arguments to make a point. But he has shown a keen appreciation of symbolic gestures, as when he stood in a mosque in Istanbul and prayed alongside his Muslim host.

In the view of several Vatican officials, his 2008 trip to the United States and the United Nations was his most

70

Journalist John Thavis questions the Pope in an interview
session aboard the papal flight to the United States, April 15, 2008.

successful to date. Its impact began
aboard the flight from Rome. Answer-
ing a reporter's question about priestly
sex abuse, the Pope spoke from his
heart about the shame, the damage to
the Church and the victims' suffering.

By the time he landed in Washington, the air was cleared and the wind
was in his sails. Over the following
days, he combined praise for the U.S.
model of church-state relations with a
probing critique of "new secularism"
and its dangers for the soul of society.
From his American audience, he got a
far more sympathetic hearing than his
aides had predicted. ■

Pope Benedict XVI arrives at Andrews Air Force
Base in Maryland, April 15, 2008.

Opposite: Pope travels in popemobile
around Yankee Stadium in 2008.

AFRICA: RECONCILIATION, JUSTICE AND PEACE

BY STEPHEN R. HILBERT

Since the start of his pontificate, Pope Benedict XVI has made Africa a priority. He recognizes that the Church in Africa is the fastest growing local Church in the world, but also the poorest materially. The Church in Africa ministers to a land of great promise and peril.

In December 2008, the Pope prayed for the people of the Democratic Republic of Congo, Darfur, particularly Sudan, and Somalia, whose "sufferings are the tragic consequence of the lack of stability and peace." He reiterated his concern for these war-torn countries in a 2009 address, urging leaders on the national and international levels to do everything necessary "to resolve the current conflicts and to put an end to the injustices which caused them." At the United Nations, the Holy See has highlighted how poverty threatens peace and stability in the world community.

Most importantly, the Pope made 2009 a de facto Year of Africa through three significant actions.

First, in March, he visited Africa. In 17 homilies and addresses over six days, he preached hope and responsibility for the future. In Yaoundé, he declared that the duty of Christians, particularly laypeople with economic or political responsibilities, is "to be guided by the Church's social teaching, in order to contribute to the building up of a more just world where everyone can live with dignity."

Second, during his trip to Africa, he released the working document to be used for the October 2009 Synod on Africa. The document focused on "The Church in Africa in Service to Reconciliation, Justice and Peace" and challenged the Church not to withdraw into itself, but rather to serve a "more prophetic role" in the social and political life of the continent, with lay faithful working to

Pope Benedict XVI greets representatives from Cameroon's Baka tribe before leaving for Angola, March 20, 2009.

Previous: Aboriginal dancers perform for Pope Benedict XVI during a welcoming ceremony at World Youth Day in Sydney, Australia, July 17, 2008.

transform African societies from the  inside out.

Writing after his return from Africa, the Pope said, "Africa is a young continent, full of the joy of life and confidence, with great creative potential."

Third, the "Year of Africa" culminated in the Synod on Africa in October 2009. It was a time for the bishops of Africa to draw inspiration from their cultural values of "respect for elders; a respect for women as mothers; a culture of solidarity, mutual aid, hospitality and unity; a respect for life, honesty, truth, keeping one's word" (Working Document, March 2009).

The same year in Cameroon, the Pope urged the bishops to have courage.

"In the face of suffering or violence, poverty or hunger, corruption or abuse of power, a Christian can never remain silent," he said, adding, "The bishop's mission leads him to be the defender of the rights of the poor." ∎

Above: Children welcome the Pope to Cameroon, March 17, 2009.

Opposite: A young woman holds a sign in Portuguese welcoming the Pope to Angola, March 22, 2009.

A Continental Mission: Stand for the Poor

BY ALLAN F. DECK, SJ

In May 2007, Pope Benedict XVI traveled to Brazil to inaugurate the Fifth General Conference of the Bishops of Latin America and the Caribbean. Of the five Latin American General Conferences that have been held, three others have been inaugurated by a pope: the Conference at Medellín (1968) by Pope Paul VI, and the Conferences at Puebla (1979) and Santo Domingo (1992) by Pope John Paul II.

The lead-up to Pope Benedict's arrival in Aparecida, Brazil, found considerable speculation regarding the direction he would take on at least two major issues: (1) Would he confirm the Latin American bishops' historical commitment to a somewhat inductive see-judge-act method for pastoral planning, or would he stress the importance of a more deductive approach that begins with the Church's received teachings and traditions? (2) Would he reaffirm the Church's preferential option for the poor in the spirit of the three previous General Conferences?

In his remarks, Pope Benedict implicitly acknowledged the inductive method used by the bishops to analyze the reality of the faithful.

Pope Benedict specifically raised the issue of the preferential option for the poor. He reconfirmed it in the clearest possible way and added his own theological emphasis in doing so. In the inaugural address, for example, he said that "the preferential option for the poor is implicit in the Christological faith in the God who became poor for us, so as to enrich us with his poverty."

All in all, Pope Benedict XVI's participation at Aparecida was well received and contributed to the Conference's central message, the "continental mission," which stresses the call given to all the faithful to be missionary disciples of Jesus Christ. ∎

The Pope embraces children of the Fazenda da Esperança (Farm of Hope) in Guaratinguetá, Brazil, May 12, 2007. The Farm of Hope community provides rehabilitation services for those addicted to drugs and alcohol.

Pope Benedict XVI looks on as young people present gifts of dark bread, light bread, rice, unleavened bread and maize, representing the five continents during a rally at St. Joseph Seminary in Yonkers, N.Y., April 19, 2008.

With Youth: Ever the Catechist

BY SISTER EILEEN MCCANN, CSJ

Saying, "With great joy I welcome you, dear young people," Pope Benedict XVI signaled his intention to carry on the legacy of Pope John Paul II in reaching out to the young. In that same speech at the 2005 World Youth Day, Pope Benedict gave tribute to the great work of Pope John Paul II among young people: "Now all of us together have to put his teaching into practice."

Fortunately, Pope Benedict's style lends itself to this mission. During World Youth Days from Cologne to Yonkers to Sydney, young people have come to expect deep challenges from Pope Benedict XVI. "Where is the One who can offer me the response capable of satisfying my heart's deepest desires?" he asked youth in Cologne. "Asking such questions also means searching for Someone who can neither deceive nor be deceived, and who therefore can offer a certainty so solid that we can live for it and, if need be, even die for it."

"Dear young people, let me now ask you a question," he probed in Sydney in 2008. "What will you leave to the next generation?... Are you living your lives in a way that opens up space for the Spirit in the midst of a world that wants to forget God, or even rejects him in the name of a falsely-conceived freedom?" And in his 2009 World Youth Day message, Pope Benedict XVI focused on hope, acknowledging that youth is a special time of hope. He urged them to accept Jesus as "your hope" and to "communicate this to others with your joy and your spiritual, apostolic and social engagement."

The young people's exuberant cheers show their acceptance of Pope Benedict XVI. He, too, has grown more comfortable with them, even reaching out through digital media such as YouTube and sending inspirational text messages to young people during World Youth Day in Sydney.

Pope Benedict XVI, delighting in young people, offers them a picture of Jesus who both challenges and offers hope. This is the legacy he exhorts young people to leave to the next generation. ■

A Father with His Children

CARDINAL FRANCIS GEORGE, OMI • ARCHBISHOP OF CHICAGO

DURING POPE BENEDICT'S VISIT to the United States, every moment was programmed, every event scheduled, every person instructed so that everything came together as planned and as necessary. Watching the visit unfold hour by hour within the net of security and the prescriptions of the Pope's staff was fascinating; but even more fascinating was watching the Pope as he broke out, at odd moments, to respond to those who had come to see him.

He responded with unexpected spontaneity to the seminarians and young religious at Dunwoodie Seminary in New York. He responded with quiet tenderness to the disabled children and their parents and caregivers in the seminary chapel, taking time to be personally present to each person in ways that he or she might be able to grasp. Early on in his visit, he responded with good humor to the children who had come to greet him as he left the Apostolic Nunciature to begin the day's program.

Children from the Catholic schools of the Archdiocese of Washington had gathered outside the Nunciature to greet the Pope as he began his visit. He would not have time to come to any school, so they came to him. It was his birthday, and they sang "Happy Birthday" in German! The Pope stopped as he came down the stairs and looked at the children, mostly African American and Hispanic. Then he went to them and greeted them, telling them how exact their German pronunciation was. He left his entourage waiting until he had greeted them all, a father with his children, each going out of his or her way to honor the other.

---

nd the Church is young. She holds within herself the future of the world and therefore shows each of us the way towards the future.

—*Homily, inaugural Mass, April 24, 2005*

The Pope greets children with disabilities at St. Joseph Seminary in Yonkers, N.Y., April 19, 2008.

Papal Visit 2008: Christ Our Hope

BY HELEN OSMAN

It could have been a perfect storm: the first visit by the only truly international religious leader to the United States since 9/11, and the first visit by a pope with a reputation in some circles as "the enforcer" since the clergy sex abuse crisis of the Catholic Church in the United States. But the first visit of Pope Benedict XVI to the United States was instead something of a family reunion, filled with love, laughter and tears of joy.

Despite attempts by some, before Pope Benedict's April 15-20 visit, to frame it as an opportunity for the Pope to berate his American flock, the event provided him with an opportunity to show what he does best: be a strong pastoral leader, a gentle shepherd, a loving yet engaged grandfather.

Even before setting foot at Andrews Air Force Base in the Washington, D.C., area, Pope Benedict set the tone for the trip when he unflinchingly answered reporters' questions on the flight, saying that he was "deeply ashamed" of the sexual abuse perpetrated by clergy. His texts throughout the trip, as well as the visual images he presented to the public, made it clear that he had great admiration for the United States, while encouraging Catholics in the United States to "go deeper" into their faith.

With President and Laura Bush, Pope Benedict greets the crowd from a porch overlooking the South Lawn of the White House, April 15, 2008.

And Americans responded with love and affection to his gentle challenge. The visit received an astonishing 16 percent of the available "news hole" in U.S. media. It was second in coverage on television (both cable and network news), on radio and in newspapers—only behind one of the most dramatic presidential primary seasons—and it was first in online news.

Perhaps more telling, most media got out of the way and allowed the public to meet Pope Benedict in a more intimate way.

Two national polls, including one by the Pew Research Center, showed that the Pope received a 10-point bump in favorability among Americans because of the visit.

Pope Benedict impressed and surprised many, but perhaps most especially he surprised the media. An April 20, 2008, blog post by Fox News' Lauren Green sums it up well: "On Tuesday, we didn't know what to expect when he stepped off the plane. Now that we've seen him—the Shepherd One, this German nicknamed 'God's Rottweiler'—and heard his voice, witnessed his smile and incredible humility, he has become someone so close to us all." ■

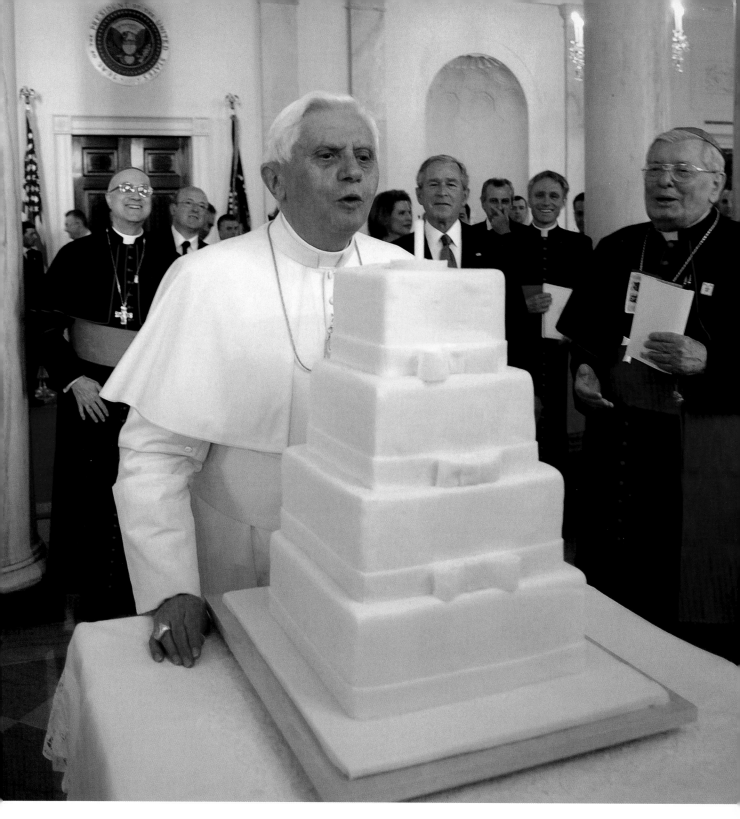

Pope Benedict XVI blows out a candle on a birthday cake presented to him at the White House, April 16, 2008, when he turned 81. His birthday took place on the second day of his U.S. visit.

Opposite: Pope Benedict XVI gives Communion to a U.S. soldier during Mass at Nationals Park in Washington, April 17, 2008.

Seen Through the Camera Lens

NANCY WIECHEC • VISUAL MEDIA MANAGER, CATHOLIC NEWS SERVICE

ONE THING I NOTICED about Pope Benedict that really makes an impression is how he looks everyone he meets right in the eye and lingers there. He seems keenly aware of each person and everything going on around him. That makes him very personable, even though he must greet hundreds of individuals each month. After I photographed his 2008 U.S. visit, a fellow journalist asked me how I would describe the Pope. I saw him like this: a senior but energetic professor, who still wants to guide his students through the lessons of life.

Above: The Pope enters Nationals Park, where he celebrated Mass, April 17, 2008.

Opposite: Pope Benedict XVI prays at the site of the destroyed World Trade Center towers in New York, April 20, 2008. He spoke with family members of some of the victims of the 2001 terrorist attacks and with some first responders to the disaster.

Following: The Pope walks toward the altar for Mass in Yankee Stadium, April 20, 2008.

Right Church, Wrong City

SISTER MARY ANN WALSH, RSM • DIRECTOR OF MEDIA RELATIONS, USCCB

WHEN TRAVEL-WEARY Pope Benedict visited the Archdiocese of New York in April 2008, he agreed to record a greeting for The Catholic Channel, the archdiocese's enterprise on Sirius Satellite Radio. Joe Zwilling, head of The Catholic Channel, offered the Pope the opportunity to work from a prepared script or to ad-lib his remarks. The Holy Father, who visits magnificent churches wherever he goes, decided to ad-lib and began to speak about St. Patrick's Cathedral in Washington. The recording session stopped as the Pope recognized his error in putting the famed church in the wrong city. He reached for his prepared remarks to start over, took a beat, looked up and with perfect comedic timing declared, "Well, at least I didn't say I was at Notre Dame in Paris!"

Pope Benedict XVI gives Communion to a member of the Missionaries of Charity during Mass at St. Patrick's Cathedral in New York, April 19, 2008.

Opposite: Bishops of the United States process into St. Patrick's Cathedral, New York City, where the Pope celebrated Mass with clergy and religious, April 19, 2008.

He Wanted to Be There

HELEN OSMAN, SECRETARY FOR COMMUNICATIONS • UNITED STATES CONFERENCE OF CATHOLIC BISHOPS

I COULD NOT sit or stand still on the grandstands at Andrews Air Force Base on April 15, 2008. The Pope was due to arrive at any minute. I probably hadn't slept more than three hours a night for weeks, as we crammed what was usually 18 months of preparation for a papal visit into less than six months. Now the plane was on the ground, and we were waiting for the door to open. The buzz and anticipation among the crowd were palpable. Then someone appeared at the doorway. A somewhat small, white-robed figure literally bounded down the steps. He was obviously delighted, excited, waving at the crowds, who were wildly cheering. It's like a grandfather coming to see his family, I thought. Forget the "Rottweiler" image, folks. And I knew, no matter what snags we might have in the days ahead, the rest of the visit would be wonderful. He wanted to be here. We wanted him to be here. It would be a great family reunion.

Children welcome the Pope during his 2008 visit to the United States.

Opposite: Youth gather at St. Joseph's Seminary in Yonkers, N.Y., to greet the Pope on April 19, 2008.

PART II PASTOR

GIVING THE LOOK OF LOVE THEY CRAVE

BY MARIA DEL MAR MUÑOZ-VISOSO

ope Benedict XVI has made *caritas*, love, a preferred theme and a main cause of his pontificate.

The first encyclical letter of his pontificate, *God Is Love* (*Deus Caritas Est*), best summarizes his teachings in this area. His third encyclical, *Charity in Truth* (*Caritas in Veritate*), a social encyclical, also contains much wisdom on this topic.

In *God Is Love*, the Pope reminded us that "God's love for us is fundamental for our lives, and it raises important questions about who God is and who we are" (no. 2). Since God has loved us first (see 1 Jn 4:10), love is now no longer a "command"; it is the response to the gift of God's love.

For Pope Benedict, love encompasses the whole of human existence. Man needs to both give love and receive it as a gift. The eucharistic communion, he said, includes the reality both of being loved and of loving others in turn. "A Eucharist which does not pass over into the concrete practice of love is intrinsically fragmented," he said (*God Is Love*, no. 14).

An "intimate encounter with God" leads to a "communion of will" in which we learn to look at the other person from the perspective of Jesus Christ.

More recently, in *Charity in Truth*, Pope Benedict reminded us that charity without truth is mere sentimentalism and that love in truth "is the principal driving force behind the authentic development of every person and of all humanity" (no. 1).

For many, Pope Benedict's act of opening his pontificate with an encyclical on love was not only a wise move but a true "act of love" for the Church.

The question of love is so fundamental to human existence that the Pope did not hide in the opening statements the reason for this letter, *God Is Love*, which would set the tone of his pontificate: "to speak of the love which God lavishes upon us and which we in turn must share with others" (no. 1). ∎

Opposite: Pope Benedict XVI meets with a young boy, Oct. 22, 2009.

Previous: The Pope walks in St. Peter's Square, Dec. 1, 2008.

TEACHER

ARCHBISHOP TIMOTHY DOLAN • ARCHBISHOP OF NEW YORK

"HE'S A TEACHER," I always reply when someone asks my impression of Pope Benedict XVI. In one way, of course, we can say that of any successor of Peter, the Prince of the Apostles, since Jesus sent his first apostles "to teach."

But Benedict XVI is a teacher, a professor, not only in his *supernatural* task as pastor of the Church Universal, but in a wonderfully *natural* way, as the *grace* of his office builds on a *nature* wonderfully talented to evangelize the world.

His theological acumen, admired for decades, gives him a depth, a profound grasp of the truth as imparted by *the Teacher*, Jesus, wrestled with by reason and handed on lovingly and tenderly by his Church.

I remember meeting with Pope Benedict while he was still Cardinal Joseph Ratzinger, and I was impressed so much by how intently he listened to us visiting bishops. No wonder: a masterful teacher is first a student, a disciple.

That's "what he's like," this shy, brilliant Bavarian who has us listening eagerly to his talks and devouring his writings.

They come to Rome to listen to him, to hear him, to learn from a professor who now occupies an "endowed chair" once occupied by Peter.

Above: The Pope reads outdoors on vacation.

Opposite: The Pope walks with youth from different cultures at World Youth Day in Cologne.

fter the great Pope John Paul II, the Cardinals have elected me, a simple and humble laborer in the vineyard of the Lord. The fact that the Lord knows how to work and to act even with inadequate instruments comforts me, and above all I entrust myself to your prayers.

— First Urbi et Orbi *Blessing upon being elected pope, April 19, 2005*

The Pope prays in his chapel at Castel Gandolfo.

Following: Detail of Our Lady of Altötting, which is displayed near the sanctuary of the Basilica of the National Shrine of the Immaculate Conception in Washington, March 4, 2008. Pope Benedict stopped to pray at the statue during his visit to the shrine. This representation of Mary is revered by Catholics in Bavaria, where the original statue resides and where young Joseph Ratzinger grew up.

Turning to Altötting, Inspired by Mary

BY SISTER MARY ANN WALSH, RSM

oseph Ratzinger developed a devotion to Our Lady of Altötting, patroness of Bavaria, as a child. Her shrine, located about 12 miles from the Pope's birthplace in Marktl am Inn, has been a pilgrimage site since the 15th century. Throngs have gone there in search of miracles and comfort.

One million people visit annually. There she is known as the Black Madonna, a charred linden wood statue, darkened by centuries of candle smoke. In 2006, he left at the foot of the statue the ring he received from Pope Paul VI when he became cardinal.

Visits to Marian shrines are a part of Pope Benedict's trips to foreign lands. In France, he visited Lourdes; in Austria, Mariazell; in Poland, Częstochowa; in Brazil, Aparecida. In the United States, he met with the U.S. bishops at the Basilica of the National Shrine of the Immaculate Conception in Washington, where several oratories bear one of the titles of the Virgin. On his 81st birthday, he prayed at the shrine's oratory of Our Lady of Altötting, a gift from the German people.

The Pope holds Mary up as the model for Christians. He emphasizes her "Fiat," when she said "yes" to the Angel Gabriel's announcement that she would be the Mother of God. He points out that she shows us how to love Jesus. The Pope speaks of Mary as one who strengthens faith and changes hearts. For Pope Benedict, Mary is the exemplar of how to live and a comforter who knows and shares our joys and sorrows.

Pope Benedict eschews a pietistic approach to devotion. Yet he does not deny that Mary touches emotional needs. Speaking at Lourdes in 2008, he said: "When speech can no longer find the right words, the need arises for a loving presence. We seek the closeness not only of those who share the same blood or are linked to us by friendship, but the closeness of those who are intimately bound to us by faith. Who would be more intimate to us than Christ and his holy mother, the Immaculate One?" ■

Arms of the Man

BY SISTER MARY ANN WALSH, RSM

Pope Benedict XVI's coat of arms reveals who the Pope is with its combination of papal tradition, Augustinian theology and German lore.

At the Pope's direction, the coat of arms was designed by Italian Cardinal Andrea Cordero Lanza di Montezemolo, an expert on heraldry, who explained the design in a *L'Osservatore Romano* article.

The coat of arms includes the traditional silver and gold keys, reminiscent of the keys to the kingdom of heaven, given by Jesus to St. Peter. The gold key symbolizes the power of heaven; the silver, the power of earth.

The heraldic shield is chalice-shaped, and a headpiece tops it. For the design of his coat of arms, Pope Benedict dictated one change in tradition. Previous papal coats of arms were topped by a three-tiered crown to emphasize sacred orders, authority and Magisterium (teaching). But since popes no longer have a coronation ceremony, Pope Benedict directed that a pointed miter replace the tiara. The miter has three gold lateral bands, denoting the orders, authority and Magisterium; another band runs lengthwise to unite them.

Pope Benedict added to the bottom of his shield a white pallium, the Y-shaped woolen collar with a strip in front and in back marked with crosses. The Pope and metropolitan archbishops wear a pallium of wool as part of their liturgical dress to signify their authority as pastors of the flock and the Lord's call to the Apostles: "feed my lambs."

Pope Benedict's coat of arms resembles the heraldry he adopted as Archbishop Joseph Ratzinger of Munich and Freising. On the upper left side of the shield, as one looks at it, is the head of the Moor, a brown-skinned man with red crown, red lips and red collar. The origin is not clear, and some refer to the image as the "Ethiopian head." It originally appeared on the coat of arms of the old principality of Freising as early as 1316 and has been part of the heraldry of the bishop of Freising ever since.

Across from the Moor on the papal coat of arms is a bear, laden with a pack. It recalls the German legend that a bear attacked and killed the horse of ✠ the first bishop of Freising, St. Corbinian, on the way to Rome. Afterwards, St. Corbinian made the bear carry the saint's belongings the rest of the way.

For Cardinal Cordero Lanza di Montezemolo the bear symbolizes the beast "tamed by the grace of God," and the pack, "the weight of the episcopate."

The central element on a red background is a large gold shell. For the Pope, who did doctoral studies on Augustine, it recalls the saint's tale of coming upon a boy trying to dump the sea into a hole in the sand. The futility of the effort reminded the saint of the futility of any human being trying to fully grasp the infinity of God.

Reflecting recent papal custom, no motto graces Pope Benedict's coat of arms, though he has as his episcopal motto "*Cooperatores veritatis*," "co-workers of the truth." Cardinal Cordero Lanza di Montezemolo noted that "the absence of a motto in the Pope's arms implies openness without exclusion to all ideals that may derive from faith, hope and charity." ■

The papal coat of arms, depicted in topiary outside the Palazzo del Governatorato in Vatican City, June 3, 2006. The portions of the coat of arms common to all popes, such as the tiara and crossed keys, are planted in perennials. The portions of the coat of arms unique to the current pope are planted in annuals, matching the colors of the heraldic design as closely as possible.

THE TEACHABLE GARMENT

BY DON CLEMMER

Throughout his life, Pope Benedict XVI has faithfully executed the roles he has been given in his service to the Church. As a peritus, or advising theologian, at the Second Vatican Council, he urged on the Council's reforms. As a professor in Germany, he flexed his theological mind through his writings. As Cardinal Joseph Ratzinger at the Congregation for the Doctrine of the Faith, he ensured the doctrinal clarity and orthodoxy of the Church's teaching, as well as its teachers.

It follows then that when he became pope, Benedict XVI embraced all the conventions of his new ministry, including its dress code. This caused a splash, as some of the attire in question hadn't been seen in several decades, if not several centuries.

The ruby red papal shoes, erroneously thought to be Prada, had not adorned the feet of John Paul II during his 26-year pontificate. The camauro, the ermine-trimmed winter cap, reminiscent of Santa Claus, had not warmed a pope's head since John XXIII (1958-1963). These items along with bright-colored new vestments garnered media attention, including *Esquire*'s naming him "Accessorizer of the Year."

While some have bemoaned the focus on the Pope's fashion as trivial, Pope Benedict has managed to make it catechetical.

For instance, he hasn't revived all of the old papal dress code. The well-known beehive-shaped triple tiara, set aside by Pope Paul VI (1963-1978), was demoted yet again when Benedict removed its image from his coat of arms and replaced it with a simple bishop's miter—thus sending a strong message about his vision for his ministry via his clothes.

Another wardrobe change under Pope Benedict involved the papal pallium—the wool band worn by an archbishop over his vestments at Mass. After his election, Benedict XVI wore a redesigned pallium, one modeled

The Pope smiles for the camera in his camauro, also affectionately known as the "Santa hat."

Previous: A child meets the Pope at his summer residence in Les Combes, Valle d'Aosta, July 11, 2006.

Here Pope Benedict appears in a Saturno hat from the Vatican's collection, Sept. 6, 2006.

Opposite: Pope Benedict XVI waves to the crowd after the Papal Mass at Nationals Park, April 17, 2008.

after those used in the first millennium and depicted in mosaics around Rome. Instead of two strips of fabric hanging in the center of this garment, one at the wearer's chest and one at his back, this pallium featured longer, sashlike strips draping from the Pope's left shoulder, representing a shepherd's feed bag.

While the Pope has since returned to wearing a more conventional pallium, this was another instance of how a teacher like Pope Benedict XVI is able to use even a seemingly superficial subject like fashion to teach about the Church, the papacy, its history and its identity. ■

f it is true that death no longer has power over man and over the world, there still remain very many, in fact too many, signs of its former dominion. Even if through Easter Christ has destroyed the root of evil, he still wants the assistance of men and women in every time and place who help him to affirm his victory using his own weapons: the weapons of justice and truth, mercy, forgiveness and love.

—Easter Urbi et Orbi *Message, 2009*

A Standing Invitation

Archbishop John C. Nienstedt • Archbishop of Saint Paul and Minneapolis

MY FIRST ENCOUNTER with the man who would become Pope Benedict XVI took place in Rome while I was working at the Vatican Secretariat of State, living at the Villa Stritch, a residence of American priests.

Cardinal Joseph Ratzinger had been invited one day for lunch, or *pranzo*, the major meal of the day in Rome. I was a little late for the beginning of the meal, as our section worked a half hour longer than the other Vatican offices. I found myself at the second table, quite a way down from where the cardinal was seated. However, I was close enough to hear the conversation.

Many questions were put to his eminence, and he answered in a calm, steady voice, with insight and interest. He was soft-spoken, but I was impressed with the knowledge that he displayed on virtually every issue.

Toward the end of the meal, there was a pause in the conversation and someone asked, "Your Eminence, do you play any sports?"

He answered, "When I was in Bavaria, I often went downhill skiing. But since coming to Rome, I have no one with whom to go skiing."

Every other head in the room turned to me. "Father Nienstedt skis," a voice energetically volunteered. The cardinal looked at me expectantly.

"Your Eminence," I said, "any time you want to go, I'll drop everything and take you skiing."

Well, I waited for the call that never came. Somehow, I do not think it will now.

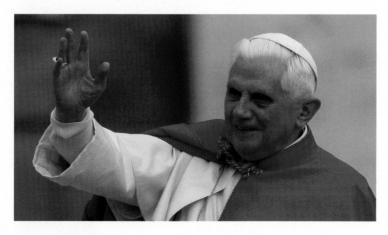

Pope Benedict XVI greets visitors at his general audience in St. Peter's Square, Nov. 21, 2007.

Opposite: Pope Benedict XVI celebrates Mass at Yankee Stadium in New York, April 20, 2008.

MUSIC:
JOY TO HIS WORLD

BY MARIA DEL MAR MUÑOZ-VISOSO

give thanks to God for having put me close to music, like a travel companion, which has always offered me consolation and joy," Pope Benedict said after a 2007 concert at the Vatican celebrating his 80th birthday.

He might be the first pope who owns an iPod, but ask Benedict XVI what the heavenly liturgy sounds like and he will probably say that it is nothing short of Mozart's Mass in C Minor, which was performed at the very concert to which his brother, Georg, took him in Salzburg, Austria, when the future pope was just 14 years old, and which has inspired both of them for the rest of their lives.

Almost 70 years later, Pope Benedict had the same Mozart composition performed in the Sistine Chapel to honor his brother, now Msgr. Georg Ratzinger, on his 85th birthday. After the concert, the Pope said that although he was only a boy, "I understood that we experienced something other than a simple concert, that it was music at prayer, the Divine Office, in which we almost could touch something of the magnificence and beauty of God himself, and we were touched."

When they were children, their parents made them play the harmonium with the view that it would prepare them for the organ. Music was a big part of their lives. "Mozart thoroughly penetrated our souls, and his music still touches me deeply because it is so luminous and yet at the same time so deep. His music is by no means just

The Pope plays the piano at his summer residence in Les Combes, Valle d'Aosta, July 17, 2006.

entertainment; it contains the whole tragedy of human existence," he said in a 1996 interview with Peter Seewald.

The Pope's favorite musical pieces are said to be Mozart's Clarinet Quintet and Clarinet Concerto. When Benedict is by himself, or in the company of a few close friends, he likes to play the piano. Although he doesn't play as often as he used to, the slower pace of summertime at Castel Gandolfo and other retreat places offers more opportunity for the Pope to pursue this "source of inspiration and serenity," as he once described music.

"We are able to hear, usually in the evening, sonatas by Mozart, Bach and Beethoven, performed by the Pope," Saverio Petrillo, director of the villa since 1986, told *L'Osservatore Romano* in 2008. "And it is something that fills us with joy because it means that Benedict XVI feels truly at home."

Music and song can help listeners reflect on the beauty and mystery of Christ, the Pope said after a concert to mark the 80th anniversary of Vatican City State (February 12, 2009), in which the choir and orchestra performed Handel's *Messiah*. "Music, like art, can be a particularly great way to proclaim Christ because it is able to eloquently render more perceptible the mystery" of the faith.

Pope Benedict has often used musical imagery to describe theological concepts. In his 2006 address on sacred music, he said, "An authentic renewal of sacred music can only happen in the wake of the great tradition of the past. . . . For this reason, in the field of music as well as in the areas of other art forms, the ecclesial community has always encouraged and supported people in search of new forms of expression without denying the past."

Cardinal Joachim Meisner of Cologne is said to have coined the term "Mozart of theology" to describe "Papa Ratzinger's" theological work. His brother, Georg, sees a certain logic to it: "Directness, clarity and form: his work seems to have these elements in common with Mozart's music" (*AD2000*, April 2006).

As he waved to the multitudes in Washington and New York in April 2008, the Pope wiggled his fingers in the air, as if playing an imaginary piano. The gesture came to be known among media as Pope Benedict's "piano fingers" greeting. The signature both betrayed his favorite pastime and signaled that the Pope, shy by nature, was now more at ease when facing the friendly crowds that were hungry for his words. ■

Pope Benedict XVI greets his brother, Msgr. Georg Ratzinger, for his 85th birthday at a concert in the Sistine Chapel, Jan. 7, 2009.

THE WORD HAS A FACE, THE PERSON, CHRIST

BY FATHER JAMES MASSA

In his first year in office, Pope Benedict XVI drew huge crowds in St. Peter's Square—even more people than his predecessor did. The saying that was often heard in Rome that first year makes a good point: "People came to *see* John Paul. They come to *listen to* Benedict."

The Church is living through one of the greatest teaching pontificates in history. As Joseph Ratzinger, the professor and prefect of the Vatican's doctrine office, Pope Benedict had a long career of studying the Scriptures and the great commentators on the Word of God. At the Second Vatican Council (1962-1965), he and Karl Rahner, SJ, were among the principal contributors to the *Constitution on Divine Revelation* (*Dei Verbum*).

He has taken issue with the Protestant principle of "Scripture alone," the idea that the Bible is the only authoritative source for what Christians should believe. He believes such teaching undervalues Tradition and makes faith depend on the always-changing findings of scholars.

At the 2008 Synod on the Word of God, Pope Benedict emphasized the inexhaustible character of God's Word. "The Word has a Face," he said; "it is a person, Christ." Modern methods of interpretation cannot finally make known *who* this divine Person is. The tools of the historian provide useful information about the times and culture in which Jesus spoke. But they cannot give us a basis on which to *believe* in him as our hope of eternal life.

No one is above the Word, not even popes and bishops, who have the sacred charge of giving definitive interpretation to it. All are called to the obedience (*oboedire* in Latin) of attentive listening, after the example of Mary, the Mother of God, in whom the "Word became flesh." By our love, by our service to our brothers and sisters, that same Word becomes a powerful testimony in our lives, much as it has in the faith-filled journey of Pope Benedict XVI. ■

Pope Benedict XVI reviews a book in his library at Castel Gandolfo, Aug. 18, 2006.

Still Witnessing at the Empty Tomb

CARDINAL JOHN FOLEY • GRAND MASTER OF THE ORDER OF THE HOLY SEPULCHRE OF JERUSALEM

AFTER HE APPOINTED ME Grand Master of the Order of the Holy Sepulchre of Jerusalem, Pope Benedict XVI kindly invited me to accompany him during his visit to the Holy Land. For me, a very memorable moment was when he faced the entrance to the Holy Sepulchre and he said that, like St. Peter, he was looking at the empty tomb and giving witness to the Resurrection of Jesus. He also thanked our Order of the Holy Sepulchre for all that the members have done for the Christians in the Holy Land. The most touching moment of the trip, however, was—in the quiet of Mount Calvary—seeing the Holy Father kneeling in silent prayer for almost 15 minutes at the spot where Jesus died and from which he was taken to his tomb just a few yards away. It is said that one of the most powerful arguments for religion is a strong man on his knees—and the Pope kneeling in silent prayer at the place of the Crucifixion of Jesus is in itself a powerful sermon.

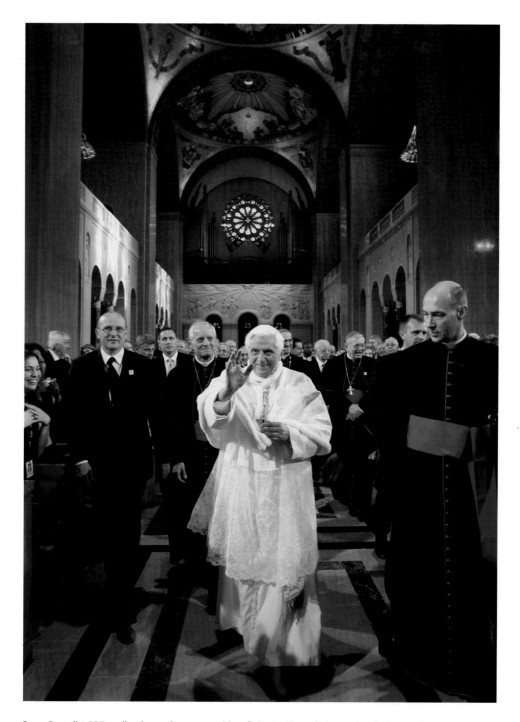

Pope Benedict XVI walks down the center aisle of the Basilica of the National Shrine of the Immaculate Conception to meet with the bishops of the United States, April 16, 2008, in Washington.

Opposite: The Pope takes a stroll in the gardens on the Vatican grounds, May 5, 2005.

Pope Benedict XVI blesses the altar with incense at the celebration of Vespers at the Basilica of the National Shrine of the Immaculate Conception, where he met with the U.S. bishops, April 16, 2008, in Washington.

Pope Benedict XVI, Model Liturgist

BY MSGR. ANTHONY SHERMAN

ope Benedict XVI has a passionate devotion to the liturgy. This was evident even before he became pope, when he wrote his well-known work *The Spirit of the Liturgy*. It showed subsequently in his apostolic exhortation *The Sacrament of Charity* (*Sacramentum Caritatis*), the document following the Synod on the Eucharist, and then nine months later in his encyclical *On Christian Hope* (*Spe Salvi*). All of these writings invite Catholics into a deeper understanding of the liturgy.

Pope Benedict desires to lead others to draw from the tremendous riches found in the liturgical celebration. Many of his homilies draw from Scripture, the Church Fathers and Tradition to evoke a deeper appreciation of the full, active and conscious participation in the liturgy as set forth by the Second Vatican Council.

On June 28, 2008, in a homily on the Feast of Sts. Peter and Paul, the Pope provided a description of himself based on Romans 15, where Paul described himself as apostle to the Gentiles. Pope Benedict described his own vocation "to serve as liturgist of Jesus Christ for the nations." The ultimate goal is for the world in all its parts to become a liturgy of God. The world's main purpose, he said, is to offer adoration to God; only in this way will it find true fulfillment.

Pope Benedict addresses the pastoral issues of the day. In a gentle but insistent way, he spoke to the youth in Cologne, Germany, for World Youth Day on declining Mass attendance. He challenged the youth to pledge themselves to the Sunday celebration of the Eucharist, and he reminded them that "it is not we who are celebrating for ourselves, but it is the living God himself who is preparing a banquet for us." Revisiting this topic in a meeting with children who had received their First Communion, he actually provided them with words they could use if they needed to urge their parents to take them to Mass.

The Holy Father has also personally urged the completion of the translation

of the *Roman Missal* into English and even entered into the discussion of the translation of the words of Consecration and the Eucharistic Prayer himself.

In other expressions of concern for the liturgy, he issued *Summorum Pontificum* (July 7, 2007) to try to accommodate those who prefer Mass in Latin by allowing use of the preconciliar liturgical form. Recently, he has initiated a discussion about the placement of the sign of peace in the Mass. Such matters are important to Pope Benedict XVI, who holds up the liturgy as a precious diamond that has many facets that he seeks to constantly and consistently reveal to the Church. ■

aith, hope and charity go together. Hope is practiced through the virtue of patience, which continues to do good even in the face of apparent failure, and through the virtue of humility, which accepts God's mystery and trusts him even at times of darkness. Faith tells us that God has given his Son for our sakes and gives us the victorious certainty that it is really true: God is love!

—God Is Love (Deus Caritas Est), no. 39

Pope Benedict XVI celebrates Mass at St. Patrick's Cathedral in New York City.

WORSHIP AND MINISTRY UNITE

ARCHBISHOP GEORGE J. LUCAS • ARCHBISHOP OF OMAHA

I HAVE ALWAYS had the experience that Pope Benedict XVI communicates very powerfully his pastoral care for the Church when he celebrates the sacred liturgy. This was evident at World Youth Day in Cologne soon after he became pope, as well as during his visit to the United States in 2008. I experienced it very profoundly during the Mass on the Feast of Sts. Peter and Paul, when the pallium was imposed on the new archbishops and I was among them. We often make a practical, but false, distinction between worship and pastoral work. In the ministry of the Holy Father, there is no such distinction. During the liturgy, his manner, his voice, his words all reflect the heart of the Good Shepherd, whose only desire is to bring us safely home to the house of our Father.

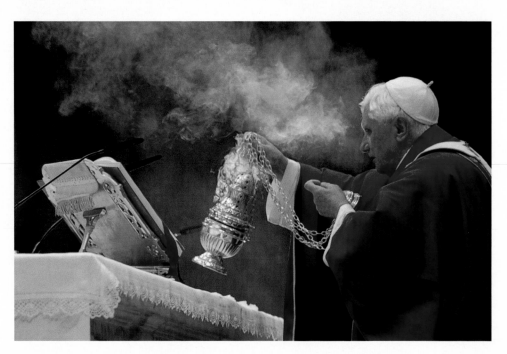

Above: Pope Benedict XVI blesses the book of the Gospels with incense during Mass on the fourth anniversary of John Paul II's death, April 2, 2009.

Opposite: Pope Benedict XVI looks at confetti falling during a meeting with youth prior to his Angelus prayer in Genoa, Sunday, May 18, 2008.

Previous: Pope Benedict XVI elevates a monstrance containing the Eucharist at the World Youth Day vigil at Royal Randwick Racecourse in Sydney, Australia, July 19, 2008.

MASS PARTICIPATION
FROM WITHIN

BY FATHER RICHARD HILGARTNER

Pope Benedict XVI, both a teacher and a celebrant of the sacraments, understands well the Second Vatican Council's well-known words about the liturgy: the "Church earnestly desires that all the faithful be led to that full, conscious, and active participation in liturgical celebrations which is demanded by the very nature of the liturgy" (*Constitution on the Sacred Liturgy* [*Sacrosanctum Concilium*], no. 14).

The reform of the liturgy has been built on this tenet, and Pope Benedict has called attention to an essential but sometimes forgotten aspect of liturgical participation: all external forms of participation in the celebration of the Mass and the other sacraments are secondary to the interior participation of our hearts in the life of Jesus Christ. Many of the Pope's writings on the liturgy have focused on the people's active interior participation, which is the meaning of "conscious participation."

In his teaching and his writings even before his election as Successor of Peter, Pope Benedict emphasized that participation in the celebration of the Mass is a participation in the work of Christ. Everything about the liturgical celebration, from words, gestures and particular roles to sacred art and sacred music, are meant to lead all—the priest celebrant and the gathered assembly—to encounter Christ and participate in his saving acts. All of these contribute to what Pope Benedict and the 2005 Synod of Bishops called the *ars celebrandi*, the "art of proper celebration."

At the start of the Eucharistic Prayer in the Mass, the priest invites all to join in the prayer: "Lift up your hearts." This is a call to interiorize the liturgy, to make it our own, so that our words and actions in prayer represent and express the faith and devotion of our hearts. Pope Benedict teaches that this is at the heart of the *ars celebrandi*. This lifting up—or giving over—of our hearts to Christ is what enables our par-

Local Catholics present the eucharistic gifts at Mass in Amman, Jordan, May 10, 2009.

ticipation in the real work of the liturgy, which is not the action of the priest or the action of the assembly, but the work of Christ himself. This is the real aim of the liturgy, as Pope Benedict explained in the apostolic exhortation *The Sacrament of Charity* (*Sacramentum Caritatis*): "The Church's great liturgical tradition teaches us that fruitful participation in the liturgy requires that one be personally conformed to the mystery being ✠ celebrated, offering one's life to God in unity with the sacrifice of Christ for the salvation of the whole world" (no. 64).

The ongoing work of the reform of the liturgy, which Pope Benedict XVI continues to encourage, aims to lead the Church—the priests and the faithful alike—to be more closely conformed to Christ through such "full, conscious and active participation" in worship. ■

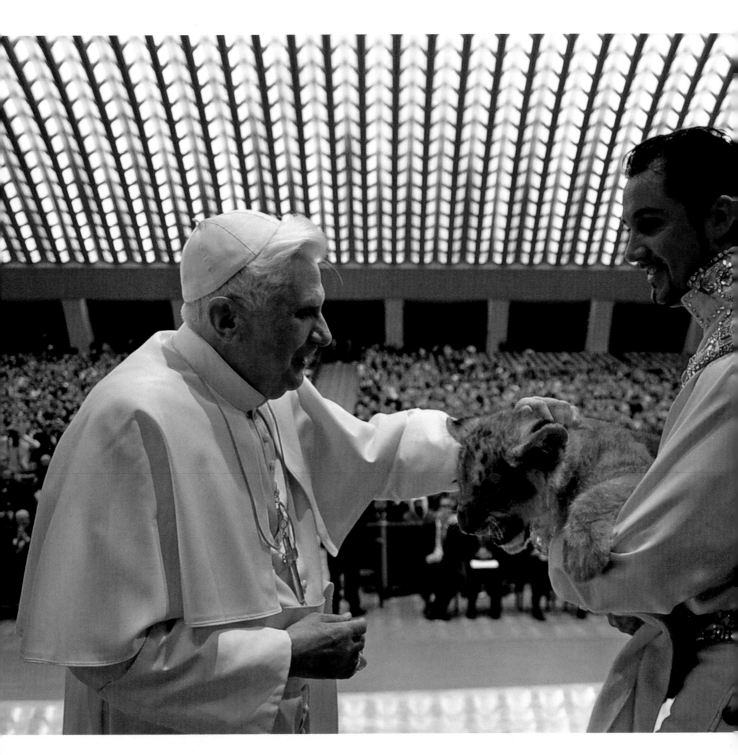

Pope Benedict XVI pets a lion cub held by a performer of the Medrano Circus during his weekly general audience at the Vatican, Jan. 28, 2009.

SHEPHERDING CATS

BY DON CLEMMER

 hortly after Pope Benedict XVI was elected, the world scrambled for a better understanding of the new pontiff. Media flocked to anyone with a personal connection. These people spoke of his gentleness, his humility, his brilliant mind. And they talked about his love of cats.

The idea that the new pope is a cat person was irresistible, sparking conflicting coverage in the first weeks of his pontificate. Some reports had him moving two cats into the papal apartments. Others had two cats being refused due to a no-pets policy in the Vatican, forcing the new pope to keep them in his old apartment. Others quoted his housekeeper as saying that Pope Benedict didn't even own a cat, but that he fed and cared for strays.

Cardinal Tarcisio Bertone, Vatican secretary of state, told the media stories of the former Cardinal Ratzinger talking to cats, cats following him from his apartment to his office, and Swiss Guards joking that his cats were laying siege to the Vatican.

While the northern Italians have furnished the Pope with a cat when he vacations there, the papal apartments are apparently cat-free. But back in his native Germany, the neighbor who cares for the Pope's old house owns a cat named Chico, who is reportedly fond of the Pope.

In fact, a cat named Chico is the narrator of the 2007 children's book *Joseph and Chico: The Life of Pope Benedict XVI as Told by a Cat*. The book features an introduction

by the Pope's personal secretary, Msgr. ✠
Georg Ganswein, who asserts that everything in the book is true.

Whether he owns one or not, Pope
Benedict's love of cats is a humanizing
quality in a world where it's challenging to find areas of common ground.
Sometimes common ground has whiskers and a tail. The Pope's ministry
is after all about unifying, as well as
shepherding. But then the leader of
the world's billion Catholics probably
knows all about the challenges of shepherding cats. ■

*Love is indeed "ecstasy," not in the
sense of a moment of intoxication,
but rather as a journey, an ongoing
exodus out of the closed inward-looking self
towards its liberation through self-giving, and
thus towards authentic self-discovery and
indeed the discovery of God....*

—God Is Love (Deus Caritas Est), *no. 6*

The Pope enjoys a moment with St. Bernard dogs
and their keepers during a visit to the Maison of
St. Bernard in Martigny, Swiss Alps, July 19, 2006.

A Bruised Knee He Shall Not Bend

CARDINAL EDWARD EGAN • ARCHBISHOP EMERITUS OF NEW YORK

ON THE DAY of his election as Supreme Pontiff, each of the cardinal electors approached Pope Benedict XVI to promise obedience, loyalty and respect. At the time I was having some trouble with my left knee, a situation that was happily corrected some months later.

As I drew near to the Successor of St. Peter, he took hold of my hands and told me that during the conclave he had noticed that I was limping. "I am sorry for your pain," he said. "Be assured that you have a special place in my prayers."

When I returned to my seat in the Sistine Chapel, the cardinal next to me asked what had happened. "I tried to make a fervent declaration of filial devotion," I answered, "and he replied with a gentle lesson in paternal love and concern."

A year later, I was at a papal audience in the Nervi Auditorium. As I bent to kiss the ring of Pope Benedict XVI, he greeted me with a smile. "You are walking much better now," he observed, "and I am so very pleased."

It was a second lesson very much like the first, and neither shall I ever forget.

Pope Benedict, sporting a cast for a broken wrist, continues his vacation in Aosta in the Italian Alps in 2009.

Opposite: The Pope walks in a garden at Castel Gandolfo.

THE HEART OF A DISCIPLE

BY FATHER DAVID L. TOUPS

ope Benedict XVI knows ✠ priestly and religious vocations come from those who have the heart of a disciple, and he urges young people to radically follow Jesus. At a 2008 Mass in Genoa, he encouraged seminarians and those discerning vocations: "do not be afraid; indeed, may you feel the attraction of definitive choices, of a serious and demanding formative process. The high standard of discipleship alone fascinates and gives joy."

In order to foster discipleship among the "young Church," the Pope has encouraged church leaders to teach young people how to pray. Speaking to the bishops of the United States in April 2008, he observed, "Prayer itself, born in Catholic families, nurtured by programs of Christian formation, strengthened by the grace of the sacraments, is the first means by which we come to know the Lord's will for our lives. To the extent that we teach young people to pray, and to pray well, we will be cooperating with God's call."

The whole Church is responsible for fostering vocations, according to Pope Benedict. In his message for the 46th World Day of Prayer for Vocations, in 2009, he cited the exhortation of Jesus to his disciples to pray that the Lord sends laborers for his harvest, and he said it resonates for the whole Church today. "Pray!" he wrote. "The urgent call of the Lord stresses that prayer for vocations should be continuous and trusting."

The Pope has confidence that when youth meet Jesus in prayer, hearts of disciples will be formed.

"Dare to dedicate your life to courageous choices, not alone of course, but with the Lord!" he said at a Mass in Savona, Italy, in May 2008. The words echoed his call at Yankee Stadium, when he exclaimed: "Young men and women of America, I urge you: open your hearts to the Lord's call to follow him in the priesthood and the religious life. Can there be any greater mark of love than this: to follow in the footsteps of Christ, who was willing to lay down his life for his friends (cf. Jn. 15:13)?" ∎

The Pope greets priests, seminarians and brothers in America at St. Joseph's Seminary in Yonkers, N.Y.

QUAERERE DEUM, TO SEEK GOD

BY SISTER JANICE BADER, CPPS

ook to the name he chose to understand Pope Benedict XVI's regard for religious life. He selected as his patron St. Benedict, the fifth-century abbot and father of Western monasticism whose influence penetrates religious life even today.

In his Angelus reflection on July 10, 2005, the Pope spoke of St. Benedict's only aim: *Quaerere Deum*, to seek God. This is the wholehearted quest of Pope Benedict's own life, but he challenges everyone, and in particular religious, to live with this singleness of heart.

When Pope Benedict visited the United States in April 2008, religious were among those who joined him in the celebration of the Eucharist at St. Patrick's Cathedral. In his homily, the Pope voiced his fraternal love for religious: "You, dear men and women religious, both contemplative and apostolic, have devoted your lives to following the divine Master in generous love and complete devotion to his Gospel." Pope Benedict looked upon the gathered religious as persons deeply committed to seeking God. He encouraged them to "prepare a path for the Spirit" through the personal witness of their lives and fidelity to the apostolate.

Religious are called to renounce everything to follow Christ, and Pope Benedict sees this as a much-needed "sign of contradiction" in our consumer society. He views communal life as another element that lights the path toward God. It provides a witness in the face of the individualism that often blocks the road to the common good. Through sharing in common and supporting one another, religious witness to the selfless love and unity that is the Trinity.

Pope Benedict affirms that those who answer the call to consecrated life are responding to the initiative of God, the God who first loved us. Vowed religious, he said at the 11th World Day of Consecrated Life in 2007, seek to satisfy "a unique thirst for love which can be quenched by the Eternal One alone." It's the response to *Quaerere Deum*—to seek only God. ■

Sister Janet Baxendale, SC, reads the Scriptures during the Pope's Mass at St. Patrick's Cathedral in New York, April 19, 2008.

PRIESTHOOD ROOTED IN PRAYER

BY FATHER DAVID L. TOUPS

St. Benedict chose "*ora et labora*" (pray and work) as the motto of his monastic community. This could also be the motto of his namesake, Pope Benedict XVI. On June 19, 2009, a day of priestly sanctification, Pope Benedict inaugurated the Year for Priests. The Pope believes that priestly life and ministry can only be carried out by men of intense prayer and tireless labor. Work that is not rooted in spirituality results in activism, through which a priest forgets the essence of who he is.

Pope Benedict's pastoral plan for the Church is one of spiritual renewal that must begin in the hearts of priests. On his visit to Bavaria, the Pope reminded priests that prayer life is not extraneous to pastoral ministry but is rather the "pastoral priority par excellence." Only here, he urged, "rests the secret of your true apostolic success."

From the start, Pope Benedict has reminded Catholics that they are not simply followers of a philosophy but are called into a personal, intimate, loving relationship with Jesus Christ.

This is the Good News, the core message of Christianity. If every Christian is called to a profound relationship with the living God, how much more urgent is this relationship for the priest, who is called to shepherd the faithful by word and example?

To lead the faithful closer to Christ, Pope Benedict reminded the priests of Poland to be "experts in the spiritual life." Thus, the priest must be a man of great prayer, as he said at the 2009 Chrism Mass, on "a journey in personal communion with Christ, setting before him our daily life, our successes and failures, our struggles and our joys—in a word, it is to stand in front of him." If the priest is to be the "expert in the spiritual life," he must be grounded in the basics of prayer in order to teach the faithful.

The 2009 announcement of the Year for Priests called for greater priestly holiness and invited the Church Universal to pray that these "spiritual fathers" be the men they are called to be, "blaz[ing] a trail of prayer" for all faithful and leading them into deeper communion with their Divine Savior. ■

Pope Benedict XVI celebrates Mass at Yankee Stadium in New York, April 20, 2008.

"You Have a Good Seminary"

CARDINAL JUSTIN RIGALI • ARCHBISHOP OF PHILADELPHIA

A COUPLE OF DAYS after his election, Pope Benedict XVI met a second time with the cardinals. This second meeting included also the retired cardinals who were not present in the Sistine Chapel either for the papal election or for the first encounter with the new pope. This second meeting followed the same pattern as the first one, offering each cardinal the opportunity to make a profession of faith and a promise of obedience. As I got up after kneeling before Pope Benedict for this solemn ceremony, I was surprised by how suddenly he could switch topics. I was delighted when he told me very simply, "You have a good seminary in Philadelphia!" Amazing, it seemed to me, how he could so soon relate his past experiences to his new papacy!

Despite all the evil present in our world, the words which Christ spoke to his Apostles in the upper room continue to inspire us: "In the world you have tribulation; but take courage, I have overcome the world" (Jn 16:33). Our faith in the Divine Master gives us the strength to look to the future with confidence. Dear priests, Christ is counting on you.

—Letter at the beginning of the Year for Priests, June 18, 2009

Then-Cardinal Ratzinger greets and congratulates
the newly elected Pope John Paul II, Oct. 22, 1978.

SEARING PAIN OF ABUSE

BY TERESA M. KETTELKAMP

Of all the problems Pope Benedict XVI has faced, the one felt most deeply is sexual abuse of children by clergy.

The Pope addressed the issue forthrightly in 2008 on the plane carrying him to his visit to the United States, where the extent of the problem first became clear. "I am deeply ashamed and we will do what is possible so this cannot happen again in the future," he said, adding, "It is a great suffering for the Church in the United States and for the church in general and for me personally that this could happen. . . . It is difficult for me to understand how it was possible that priests betray in this way their mission . . . to these children."

As a pastor, he met personally at the Vatican nunciature in Washington with a small group of victims/survivors, a dramatic expression of his care.

Then in early 2010, the scandal erupted in Europe. He continued to address the problem as its extent became apparent in several European nations, including his beloved Germany, in the Archdiocese of Munich and Freising, which he had once headed.

In response to the problem in Ireland, an almost entirely Catholic country, the Pope met with the country's bishops, accepted the resignation of those bishops who had dealt poorly with victim/survivors of child sexual abuse, and issued a pastoral letter to the Irish people. The depth of feeling showed he had heard their cries at the deepest level.

"You have suffered grievously and I am truly sorry," he said to victims/survivors in the letter. "I know that nothing can undo the wrong you have endured. Your trust has been betrayed and your dignity violated. Many of you found that, when you were courageous enough to speak of what happened to you, no one would listen."

To priests who abused children, he said, "You betrayed the trust that was placed in you by innocent young people and their parents, and you must answer for it before Almighty God and before properly constituted tribunals."

With increasing knowledge and understanding, and in the face of accu-

Pope Benedict XVI celebrates Mass at Nationals Park in Washington, April 17, 2008.

sations of cover-up, he criticized Ireland's bishops for not following church law. "I recognize how difficult it was to grasp the extent and complexity of the problem, to obtain reliable information and to make the right decisions in the light of conflicting expert advice," he wrote. "Nevertheless, it must be admitted that grave errors of judgment were made and failures of leadership occurred. All this has seriously undermined your credibility and effectiveness."

He wrote with a sense of realism too. He noted that "the problem of child abuse is peculiar neither to Ireland nor to the Church" and will require steady effort. He expressed a resolute hope. "No one imagines that this painful situation will be resolved quickly," he said. "Real progress has been made, yet much more remains to be done. Perseverance and prayer are needed, with great trust in the healing power of God's grace." ∎

Healing Compassion

CARDINAL SEÁN P. O'MALLEY • ARCHBISHOP OF BOSTON

PRIOR TO POPE BENEDICT XVI'S VISIT to the United States in 2008, much discussion took place about whether or not the Holy Father would address the clergy sexual abuse crisis. Once the Pope arrived, his words and actions made clear that he would not avoid this painful reality. In the midst of Pope Benedict's second day in Washington, two of my colleagues from the Archdiocese of Boston and five survivors of clergy sexual abuse gathered in the chapel at the Vatican embassy for what turned out to be a historic and pivotal meeting with the Pope. We spoke with the Holy Father about the impact of the abuse crisis and heard his message of hope and reconciliation. For many Catholics in the United States, and members of the wider community, this meeting was the high point of the papal visit and one of the Holy Father's most important actions.

During our very prayerful and emotional encounter with the Holy Father, we were blessed with an extraordinary opportunity to witness Pope Benedict not only as the leader of our Church, but as our pastor. The Holy Father took care to address each person individually and provided the survivors the time to speak freely. It was evident that at times they shared their painful experiences in a whisper. The Holy Father listened intently, often clasping the survivors' hands, and responded tenderly and reassuringly. One of the survivors, unable to find words, conveyed her heartache through tears that spoke volumes with her sounds of sorrow. Though we would not hear the Pope's private conversation with the woman, by observing her moving from tears to a calmed, smiling expression, we knew that the Pope had gently comforted her. Later that day, she shared with us that the Holy Father had offered his congratulations on learning that she would soon be married. In doing so, the Holy Father helped her to experience a healing moment and to see a future that would hold the promise of renewed hope and joy.

Opposite: Pope Benedict XVI talks with a survivor of clerical sexual abuse from the Archdiocese of Boston in a private meeting at the apostolic nunciature in Washington, April 17, 2008.

Following: Pope Benedict XVI blesses the crowd in St. Peter's Basilica after creating 23 new cardinals, Nov. 24, 2007.

PART III PROPHET

CARITAS IN VERITATE

BY STEPHEN M. COLECCHI

ope Benedict XVI originally planned to mark the 40th anniversary of Pope Paul VI's 1967 encyclical *On the Development of Peoples* (*Populorum Progressio*) with his own encyclical on human development in our day. In part due to the global economic crisis, he delayed issuing his work until two years later when, in 2009, he presented the world with *Charity in Truth* (*Caritas in Veritate*).

Like a parent offering encouragement to a family facing a difficult time, this teaching letter offers moral guidance to the human family facing the global economic crisis, the global ecological crisis and the scandal of global poverty.

In his third encyclical, Pope Benedict roots his teaching on human development in the love of God, *caritas*—the focus of his first encyclical, *God Is Love* (*Deus Caritas Est*)—and on truth, *veritate*—a frequent theme of his teaching and writings. Truth enables humanity to discover the authentic demands of love.

For Pope Benedict, "charity in truth" is embodied in Jesus Christ. His incarnation calls everyone to the "vocation" of human development. In *Charity in Truth*, the Pope teaches that "everything has its origin in God's love, everything is shaped by it, everything is directed towards it" (no. 2). To a world that too often has a mechanistic and utilitarian view of human life and the economy, the Pope declared in *God Is Love* that "*every economic decision has a moral consequence*" (no. 37).

This social encyclical seamlessly weaves together what many consider to be polar opposites: spirituality and human progress, "life ethics" and "social ethics," justice and charity, personal ethical behavior and more just social structures, the concerns of rich nations and the needs of poor nations. In this encyclical he has articulated a holistic vision of the human person and society in an age of globalization.

The Pope reminds humanity that the demands of love have both personal and social dimensions. Love applies to both "micro-relationships

The Pope signs his encyclical *Caritas in Veritate* at the Vatican, July 6, 2009.

(with friends, with family members ✠ or within small groups)" and "macrorelationships (social, economic and political ones)" (*Charity in Truth*, no. 2).

Pope Benedict critiques the excesses of markets that function without regard to justice (no. 35), supports increases in international assistance to poorer nations (no. 60), calls for action on the structural causes of global hunger (no. 27), champions the rights of workers (nos. 25, 32) and insists on fairer trade policies to help poor nations (nos. 33, 58).

He teaches that "*the way humanity treats the environment influences the way it treats itself, and vice versa*" (no. 51). In other words, a society that finds people expendable will find nature expendable. He declares that "a lack of respect for the right to life" weakens the "conscience of society" and its grasp of "human ecology" and thus "environmental ecology." As he observes, "The book of nature is one and indivisible" (no. 51).

Issued three days before the gathering of the leaders of the G8 nations and at a dark time of economic crisis and deepening poverty, the Pope's encyclical received widespread attention. More importantly, it focused the light of the Church's moral guidance on a path of hope for a better future for all God's children. ■

Caritas in Veritate, signed at the Vatican, July 6, 2009, is Pope Benedict's third encyclical.

Concern for the Flock

Archbishop Gregory M. Aymond • Archbishop of New Orleans

EACH TIME I HAVE MET Pope Benedict I find him most personable, and he has extremely effective eye contact. His humility has impressed me as he always asks for prayers in order that he may carry out his ministry effectively.

Most recently, I had the opportunity to meet him the day after receiving the pallium for the Archdiocese of New Orleans. I went up to him and said, "Holy Father, I bring you the affection and the respect of the people of the Archdiocese of New Orleans." Quickly, he said, "What is the situation there? Is the rebuilding continuing?" I answered his question and then he said, "Please assure them of my prayers."

Obviously, he is a man of compassion and humility. As the Successor of Peter, he remembers many things that happen in various local churches and expresses that concern.

Pope Benedict XVI reaches out to a girl at a gathering with young people with disabilities at St. Joseph Seminary in Yonkers, N.Y., April 19, 2008.

ETHICS
AND ECONOMICS

BY JOHN CARR

P ope Benedict XVI has affirmed and advanced Catholic social teaching in substantial and surprising ways, applying the Church's fundamental guidelines to the economic crisis and to the demands of charity, justice and the common good.

God Is Love (*Deus Caritas Est*) and *Charity in Truth* (*Caritas in Veritate*) outline the requirements of love of God and neighbor. These encyclicals share a common call: to prioritize the poor and vulnerable and bring an ethic of charity, justice and responsibility to economic, political, ecclesial and spiritual life.

Pope Benedict places the poor and vulnerable at the heart of the Church's mission. "Love for widows and orphans, prisoners, and the sick and needy of every kind, is as essential to [the Church] as the ministry of the sacraments and preaching of the Gospel," he declared in *God Is Love* (no. 22).

In *God Is Love*, the Pope defended traditional charity, adding that "charity must animate the entire lives of the lay faithful and therefore also their political activity, lived as 'social charity'" (no. 29). In *Charity in Truth*, he said, "Justice is inseparable from charity, and intrinsic to it. Justice is the primary way of charity" (no. 6).

Pope Benedict's social teaching transcends boundaries, demonstrating the unity of the Church's social and

Pope Benedict walks down the aisle of the UN Assembly in New York City, April 18, 2008.

✠ moral teaching, making fundamental connections between charity and truth, between the protection of life and the pursuit of justice.

Pope Benedict has articulated a distinctive Catholic environmental ethic: "The environment is God's gift to everyone, and in our use of it we have a responsibility towards the poor, towards future generations and towards humanity as a whole" (*Charity in Truth*, no. 48). He links "natural ecology" and "human ecology," connecting care for the earth and care for "the least of these."

Since Pope Leo XIII's groundbreaking encyclical *Rerum Novarum* (*On the Condition of the Working Classes*; literally, "of new things") more than a century ago, the Church has consistently defended human life and dignity; supported the rights of workers, the poor and the vulnerable; and actively pursued justice and peace. Pope Benedict strengthens and extends this tradition, responding to the "new things" of our time with compelling teaching that challenges all of us. ■

The Pope reads the Vatican newspaper, *L'Osservatore Romano.*

First Justice, Then Charity

BY KATHY SAILE

Many people serve in a soup kitchen, collect blankets and toiletries for the homeless, or volunteer at a health clinic. After a while, they begin to ask: Why are the same people in the soup line every night? Why are more families coming to the homeless shelter? Why are working people coming to the free health clinic?

These questions may lead them to work to change political or economic systems through legislative advocacy or community organizing. But the encyclicals of Pope Benedict call us to turn this process upside-down, reminding us that a central duty of our faith is to practice justice—not just direct service or almsgiving.

In *God Is Love* (*Deus Caritas Est*), Pope Benedict wrote, "Works of charity—almsgiving—are in effect a way for the rich to shirk their obligation to work for justice and a means of soothing their consciences, while preserving their own status and robbing the poor of their rights. Instead of contributing through individual works of charity to maintaining the *status quo*, we need to build a just social order in which all receive their share of the world's goods and no longer have to depend on charity" (no. 26).

In *Charity in Truth* (*Caritas in Veritate*), Pope Benedict further insisted that charity begins with justice: "If we love others with charity, then first of all we are just towards them. Not only is justice not extraneous to charity, not only is it not an alternative or parallel path to charity: justice is inseparable from charity, and intrinsic to it. Justice is the primary way of charity" (no. 6).

In both encyclicals, the Pope argued that one cannot give another charity unless one does justice first. In his call to turn upside-down one's responsibility to do works of charity and care for the poor, Pope Benedict XVI challenges us not just to address problems, but to get to the root of them. ∎

On Nov. 5, 2007, Pope Benedict celebrated Mass in St. Peter's Basilica to commemorate cardinals who died in 2007. Here, he gives his blessing, holding Pope John Paul II's staff.

HUMAN RIGHTS

BY VIRGINIA FARRIS

Human rights stand as a major concern for Pope Benedict XVI, so it was fitting that he addressed the United Nations General Assembly in April 2008 to mark the 60th anniversary of the Universal Declaration of Human Rights. He called for strengthening those rights, which are "based on the natural law inscribed on human hearts."

In his January 2007 World Day of Peace message, the Pope linked building peace to recognizing the "essential equality of human persons springing from their common transcendental dignity." That equality means that all people have the same basic rights.

In the UN address, the Pope noted that because human rights flow from natural law, they represent fundamental values that transcend different cultures and civilizations.

He described their bedrock quality and said that "the universality, indivisibility and interdependence of human rights all serve as guarantees safeguarding human dignity." He cautioned against viewing human rights in purely legal-istic terms: "Human rights . . . must be respected as an expression of justice, and not merely because they are enforceable through the will of the legislators."

Of all human rights, the Pope has emphasized the right to life at every age and condition, as well as the right to religious freedom. In the UN speech, he said freedom of religion means more than the freedom to worship. It encompasses the freedom to establish religious institutions, to conduct religious education, to express opinions and exchange information, and to influence public policies based on the moral values derived from religion. The believer, as a citizen, should have the right to choose and publicly act on his or her religious beliefs without fear.

Ultimately Pope Benedict believes that peace can only come when we respect the fundamental human rights of all people. In his UN speech, he said, "The promotion of human rights remains the most effective strategy for eliminating inequalities between countries and social groups, and for increasing security." ■

The Pope greets men and women at the UN Assembly in New York City, April 18, 2008.

HUMAN LIFE AND BIOETHICS

BY RICHARD DOERFLINGER

t the papal conclave's opening Mass in April 2005, Cardinal Ratzinger preached against "a dictatorship of relativism" ruled by "one's own ego and one's own desires." In his installation homily days later, Pope Benedict was already showing how moral absolutes serve a vision of humanity's place in a universe created by love.

"Only when we meet the living God in Christ do we know what life is," he said in his installation homily. "We are not some casual and meaningless product of evolution. Each of us is the result of a thought of God. Each of us is willed, each of us is loved, each of us is necessary."

Benedict's first encyclicals explained how our hope for a meaningful, happy life is fulfilled only by opening ourselves to serve the most defenseless. While science can help answer the question of when life begins, Pope Benedict is more concerned with each person's question about his or her own life. "Welcoming human life as a gift to be respected, protected and promoted is a commitment of everyone, all

the more so when it is weak and needs care and attention, both before birth and in its terminal phase," he said in a February 2008 Angelus message.

Pope Benedict presents not just an argument about moral norms but a vision of two attitudes towards life. One attitude asserts our egos against a meaningless or hostile world, seeking to suppress, control or manipulate other human beings if they get in the way of my goals. The other, centered in Christ, surrenders our selfish goals, accepting each life from its beginning as a gift to be nourished and defended.

In his third encyclical, *Charity in Truth* (*Caritas in Veritate*), Benedict insists that "openness to life is at the center of true development" (no. 28)—and that true environmentalism embraces a "human ecology" that defends life (no. 51).

Pope Benedict's critique of biotechnology is that, when it ignores moral limits, it does not advance humankind but asserts the power of some human beings to oppress others. In a January 2008 address, he asked,

"When human beings, in the weakest and most defenseless stage of their lives are selected, abandoned, killed or used as mere 'biological material,' how can it be denied that they are no longer being treated as 'someone' but rather as 'something,' hence, calling into question the very concept of human dignity?"

While the Church's teaching on human life is unchanging, Pope Benedict has expanded this message to illustrate how the "Gospel of Life" is simply the Gospel of Christ. ■

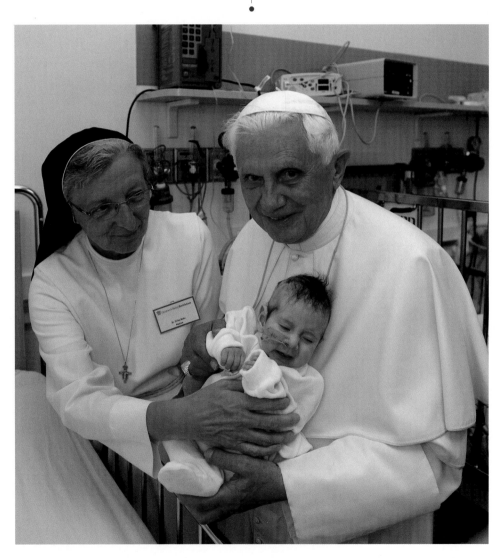

Pope Benedict XVI holds an infant at the Caritas Baby Hospital in Bethlehem, May 13, 2009.

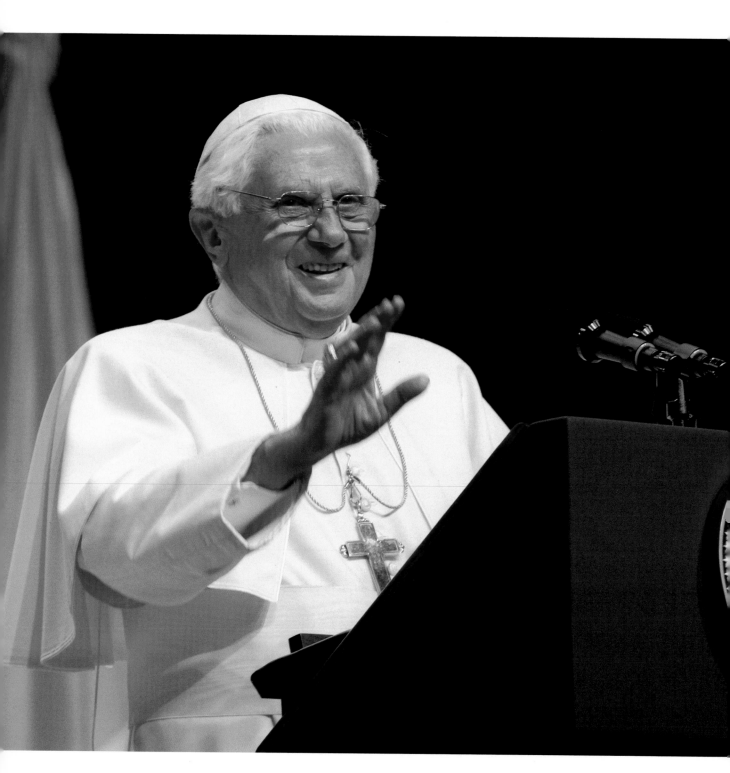

Pope Benedict XVI says farewell to America at the departure
ceremony at JFK International Airport in New York, April 20, 2008.

THE PEACE POPE

BY STEPHEN M. COLECCHI

A s a youth, Joseph Ratzinger experienced the harsh reality of war in Nazi Germany. As pope, he has dedicated his papal ministry to "the service of reconciliation and harmony between persons and peoples" (General Audience, April 27, 2005).

Pope Benedict is a "peace pope" in word and action. He proclaims the Church's teaching on peace through annual World Day of Peace messages. In his first message, he recalled choosing the name Benedict out of a "personal commitment to peace." Benedict teaches that peace is not simply the "absence of armed conflict" but is instead built on truth, justice, human rights and forgiveness. Peace is relational because human beings are loved by God and are called by God to love one another. Peace is a divine gift, but it is a human task.

Pope Benedict's rich teaching on peace touches many concerns: war, poverty, inequality, human rights, religious freedom, ecology, terrorism, disarmament, human life and the family. He relates these issues to human life and dignity, and therefore they are critical for peace.

Pope Benedict also acts for peace. In the wake of the violence that gripped southern Israel and Gaza in early 2009, he entered the Middle East as a "pilgrim of peace." The following May, standing before the wall that separates Israelis and Palestinians, he pleaded for "an end to hostilities that have caused this wall to be built" and called for "the difficult task of building peace" instead of walls.

Before the war in Iraq, then–Cardinal Ratzinger clearly stated: "The concept of a 'preventive war' does not appear in the *Catechism of the Catholic Church*." On his 2008 visit to the United States, he spoke at the White House in support of "the patient efforts of international diplomacy to resolve conflicts and promote progress." Two days later, before the United Nations General Assembly, he affirmed the UN mission to promote peace with justice and human rights.

The Pope frequently addresses urgent conflicts in every corner of the world. With his eyes fixed firmly on Christ, who is our peace, the Holy Father, in the words of his third encyclical, gives "*testimony to Christ's charity, through works of justice, peace and development*" (*Charity in Truth* [*Caritas in Veritate*], no. 15). ∎

A sign in Hebrew, English and Arabic welcomes Pope Benedict XVI to Jerusalem during his visit to the Holy Land, May 8-15, 2009.

PE BENEDICT XVI
RAEL MAY 2009
he Spirit of Unity and Peace

רושלים מברכת את

וד קדושתו בנדיקטוס ה - VI

Welcomes His Holiness Benedict X

شليم القدس ترحب بقداسة البابا بنديكتوس - ال

MIGRATION: A SIGN OF THE TIMES

BY AMBASSADOR JOHNNY YOUNG

In the *Pastoral Constitution on the Church in the Modern World* (*Gaudium et Spes*), the Second Vatican Council declared that "the Church has always had the duty of scrutinizing the signs of the times and of interpreting them in the light of the Gospel" (no. 4). Linking his papacy to this tradition, Pope Benedict XVI remarked in his 2006 World Day of Migrants and Refugees statement that "one of the recognizable signs of the times is undoubtedly migration."

The Pope understands that the decision to migrate is not simply the result of individual choice, but one that arises from factors that include economic need, political and religious persecution, and changing demands in the labor market due to globalization.

Pope Benedict has said that the Church must offer "concrete gestures of solidarity so that everyone who is far from his own country will feel the Church as a homeland where no one is a stranger" (Angelus, June 19, 2005). The Pope also calls on secular society to support and protect migrant communities.

These protections are particularly important for women and children. As more women emigrate in search of work, they are often taken advantage of, even exploited. "In some cases there are women and girls who are destined to be exploited almost like slaves in their work, and not infrequently in the sex industry," warned Pope Benedict in his 2006 statement on migrants and refugees. Unaccompanied minors can also easily fall prey to "unscrupulous exploiters who often transform them into the object of physical, moral and sexual violence," Pope Benedict said in his 2008 World Day of Migrants and Refugees Message.

While opportunity can result from migration, great dangers also confront the solitary migrant who is forced from home to find opportunity elsewhere. Pope Benedict focuses on two solutions to minimize these dangers. First, he stresses the need for family unity, since church teaching promotes support of the migrant's "family, which is

Pope Benedict XVI celebrates Mass at Yankee Stadium in New York, April 20, 2008.

a place and resource of the culture of ✠
life and a factor for the integration of
values," as he said in his 2007 World
Day of Migrants and Refugees message. Second, the Pope recognizes the
importance of creating stable societies
where opportunity is not the excep-
tion but the norm.

Pope Benedict's understanding of
migration is rooted in his conviction
that God's love extends to all people,
particularly those who are the most
vulnerable: the unaccompanied minor,
the trafficking victim, the refugee and
the migrant far from home. ■

LEADING THE GREEN REVOLUTION

BY CAROL GLATZ

rom installing solar panels on Vatican roofs to urging people to show greater care and respect for creation, Pope Benedict XVI has been leading a green revolution.

Not many expected to see him place such an emphasis on ecological concerns and become the greenest pope yet. But growing up in mountainous villages in Bavaria—where, he said in a private audience in 2006, he "experienced the beauty of creation"—nurtured his love for God's gift. Family pilgrimages to a hilltop shrine and long bike rides with his mother offered opportunities to "allow the peace of the place to have its effect on us," he said in his book *Milestones: Memoirs 1927-1977.*

In his first five years as pope, Benedict has said safeguarding the environment is a moral imperative. He has made appeals to protect the Amazon rain forest, called for greater international cooperation to reduce ozone depletion and warned of the disastrous effects of environmental degradation on the world's poor.

Through his teachings, the Pope has shown that caring for the environment is not just about protecting the air, water, land and food necessary for human survival; it is about following natural law. The first step, he has said, is to understand that God created all things, and his plan for creation must be protected. Caring for the earth and respecting one another are inextricably linked.

Just as the natural environment can be destroyed by selfishness and exploitation, he told young people in Sydney at World Youth Day 2008, so too can human life be destroyed or damaged by not recognizing human dignity and the plan God has for each person's life. In *Charity in Truth (Caritas in Veritate)*, he said that if society doesn't respect human life from conception to its natural end, "the conscience of society ends up losing the concept of human ecology and, along with it, that of environmental ecology" (no. 51). People, he has said, must live a simpler, more ethical

For his love of nature and his statements on conservation, Benedict XVI has been called the "Green Pope" by environmentalists.

177

life, curb the demand for products that ✠ harm the environment, help ensure that the world's resources are justly and equitably shared, and foster sustainable development and clean technologies in the developing world.

The Vatican has walked the talk, starting with turning the roofs of the Paul VI audience hall and the employee cafeteria into giant solar power generators. The Vatican also accepted the donation of a reforestation project in Hungary to offset the Vatican's carbon footprint, which might make Vatican City State the first carbon-neutral nation in the world. As the Pope told young people in Sydney: like the stars and the seas, the flowers and the cattle, "your very existence has been willed by God, blessed and given a purpose." As you remember to be good to Mother Earth, he tells us, don't forget your brothers and sisters. ■

The Holy Father looks out into the woods of Lorenzago di Cadore, July 19, 2007.

Opposite: In the summer of 2007, the Pope vacationed in Lorenzago di Cadore, in the Italian province of Belluno.

Betting on the Bishops

ARCHBISHOP JOSEPH A. FIORENZA • ARCHBISHOP EMERITUS OF GALVESTON-HOUSTON

IT IS CUSTOMARY for the officers of the USCCB to visit with the prefects of the Roman Curia at least twice a year. Cardinal Ratzinger always received us cordially and was prepared to discuss questions we had forwarded to him prior to the meetings. He would propose a few questions to us about statements or actions of the USCCB. The discussions were always in a fraternal spirit. His answers were thoughtful and clearly expressed. A few times he said he wanted more time to think about an issue and would give an answer on our next visit, which he always did with great kindness, even when he knew it was not the response that we had expected.

During one of the visits when the topic was the proposed document *Ex Corde Ecclesiae*, which treated the relationship of the diocesan bishop with college and universities in his diocese, Cardinal Ratzinger expressed some doubt that the U.S. bishops would approve the document. I wagered that it would pass because we were satisfied with changes that were made in the document. I wish I had put money on it because the document was approved with a sizable majority. The next time I saw Cardinal Ratzinger, he was Pope Benedict XVI and I received the pallium from him. He said to me, "Oh, I remember you." I often wondered if he remembered that he lost a bet to me.

Above: Pope Benedict XVI wears a kaffiyeh during his visit to the *Regina Pacis* (Queen of Peace) Center in Amman, Jordan, May 8, 2009.

Opposite: After Cardinal Joseph Ratzinger was elected Pope, April 19, 2005, he greeted the public from the balcony of St. Peter's.

Previous: The Pope walks in the mountains of Aosta, Italy, during his 2005 vacation.

"Friending" Is Evangelizing

BY HELEN OSMAN

espite being an introvert and an octogenarian, Benedict XVI became the first pope to make an appearance on YouTube.

Indeed, this pope has embraced new social media technology—fraught with peril and risks for an institution accustomed to measuring changes in centuries—at lightning speed. YouTube was created in 2005, the same year that the 265th pope was elected. The Vatican created a Vatican channel on YouTube in January 2009, less than four years later. The channel, *www.youtube.com/user/vatican*, offers daily news clips of the Pope with audio commentary in four languages.

Addressing pilgrims in St. Peter's Square two days after the launch, the Pope said he hoped the YouTube channel "will enrich a wide range of people—including those who have yet to find a response to their spiritual yearning—through the knowledge and love of Jesus Christ."

The wise use of online networking technology can help people form new communities "in ways that promote the search for truth, the good and the beautiful, transcending geographical boundaries and ethnic divisions," he said.

The YouTube launch was just the beginning of the Vatican's foray into what is called Web 2.0, or social media networks. On May 24, 2009, World Communications Day, it launched a new Web site, *www.pope2you.net*, specifically intended to allow users of iPhone applications and Facebook, perhaps the most dominant social networking platform in 2009, to receive and send "virtual" postcards of the Pope, along with inspiring texts from his messages.

It's not only an acknowledgment that this is perhaps the new "ends of the earth" (Mt 28:19), but also an eagerness to remind people why they find themselves drawn to the new technology. The 43rd World Day of Communications message explains: "While the speed with which the new technologies have evolved in terms of their efficiency and reliability is rightly a source of wonder, their popularity with users should not surprise us, as they respond to a fundamental desire of people to communicate and to relate to each other. This desire for communication and friendship is rooted in our very nature as human beings. . . . ✠ When we find ourselves drawn towards other people, when we want to know more about them and make ourselves known to them, we are responding to God's call." ∎

185

FAMILY: BASIS FOR SOCIETY

BY SHEILA GARCIA

estern society tends to regard marriage and family life as a private matter outside the state's interest and expertise. Attempts to strengthen the connection between marriage and family life and a healthy society often meet with suspicion.

Pope Benedict XVI vigorously challenges this thinking. Families, he has said, are the "indispensable foundation for society." The family is a school of humanity that benefits society as well as the Church. Family members coexist with each other, offer mutual support, and learn about the common good and the need for self-sacrifice. Parents teach their children to be free and responsible persons who understand that "every person is worthy of love and that there is a basic, universal brotherhood that embraces every human being," as the Pope said at the Fifth World Meeting of Families in Valencia, Spain, in 2006.

If families render this service to society, then society has a reciprocal obligation to support families. In *Char-*ity in Truth (*Caritas in Veritate*), the Pope called on governments "to enact policies promoting the centrality and the integrity of the family . . . and to assume responsibility for its economic and fiscal needs, while respecting its essentially relational character" (no. 44). Family members, he said, have the right to a home, employment, education and basic health care.

In Pope Benedict's view, anything that undermines the family undermines society. The family must be based on marriage between a man and a woman. Marriage must be open to the possibility of new life. In the face of widespread divorce and cohabitation, the Pope stresses that marriage is a permanent and faithful commitment. Finally, the family has the right to be primarily responsible for the education of its children.

In his 2008 World Day of Peace message, the Pope declared forcefully: "The denial or even the restriction of the rights of the family, by obscuring the truth about man, threatens the very foundations of peace." ■

Visitors with cellphones reach up to take photos of the Pope as he pauses to greet a child in the crowd.

FAITH AND POLITICAL LIFE

BY JOHN CARR

Pope Benedict XVI shares Catholic doctrine on faith and political life by his words and actions, as well as by what he teaches and how he applies that teaching as the leader of the universal Church. In his major documents, Pope Benedict has outlined the content of this teaching. He has demonstrated how to apply this teaching in his travels and his interactions with political leaders. He also teaches by leading the Church in defending human life and dignity, seeking justice and pursuing peace.

"It is not the Church's responsibility to make this teaching prevail in political life," Pope Benedict said in *God Is Love* (*Deus Caritas Est*). "Rather, the Church wishes to help form consciences in political life and to stimulate greater insight into the authentic requirements of justice as well as greater readiness to act accordingly . . ." (no. 28).

The Pope explicitly connects political responsibility to his call to place charity at the center of Catholic life: "charity must animate the entire lives of the lay faithful and therefore also their political activity, lived as 'social charity'" (no. 29).

On the White House lawn in April 2008, Pope Benedict described the task of Catholics in a democracy: "The preservation of freedom calls for the cultivation of virtue, self-discipline, sacrifice for the common good and a sense

Pope Benedict XVI addresses a gathering on the White House South Lawn, April 16, 2008.

of responsibility towards the less fortu- ✠
nate. It also demands the courage to
engage in civic life and to bring one's
deepest beliefs and values to reasoned
public debate."

Pope Benedict has demonstrated
these essential qualities in his five years
of service. He seeks to engage and per-
suade, addressing those who agree with
Catholic teaching and those who do
not. He has shared the moral principles and positions of the Church
at the White House and the United
Nations, with Israelis and Palestinians,
in dialogue with President George W.
Bush and President Barack Obama.
He seeks common ground and cooperation where possible and addresses
principled differences respectfully and
clearly where necessary.

Pope Benedict demonstrates in his
words and actions how the Church is
called to be political, but not parti-
san; principled, but not ideological;
civil, and still clear; engaged, but not
used. Pope Benedict practices what he
teaches on faith and political life. ■

Pope Benedict welcomes U.S. President Barack
Obama and his wife, Michelle, to the Vatican,
July 10, 2009.

A Challenge to Catholic Educators

BY MARIE A. POWELL

former theology professor at several German universities, Pope Benedict XVI has emphasized the transformative role of Catholic educational institutions. This emphasis was evident during his journey to the United States in April 2008, when he addressed Catholic educational leaders from across the United States.

Speaking to diocesan superintendents of schools and presidents of Catholic colleges and universities at The Catholic University of America, Pope Benedict proclaimed, "Education is integral to the mission of the Church to proclaim the Good News."

Pope Benedict was highly complimentary of the commitment the Church of the United States has made to education over the years, praising the generations of religious sisters, brothers, priests and others who have served the neglected and who have raised immigrants out of poverty. He urged the entire Catholic community to continue to support Catholic educational institutions so that they are accessible to persons in all economic and social strata, stating, "No child should be denied his or her right to an education in faith, which in turn nurtures the soul of a nation."

Pope Benedict challenged his audience to assess the Catholic identity of their institutions by examining how tangible the Catholic faith is in their schools, how well the faith is "given fervent expression liturgically, sacramentally, through prayer, acts of charity, a concern for justice, and respect for God's creation." He challenged educators "to evoke among the young the desire for the act of faith, encouraging them to commit themselves to the ecclesial life that follows from this belief." In this one address, Pope Benedict laid out for Catholic educational leaders in the United States a vision of Catholic education that was both encouraging and challenging: that of spreading the faith through prayer, personal witness and building institutions that form disciples of Christ. ■

Young people representing Catholic schools greet the Pope at St. Joseph Seminary in Yonkers, N.Y., April 19, 2008.

HOPE FOR TODAY

BY THOMAS G. WEINANDY, OFM CAP

"In hope we are saved" (Rom 8:24). So begins Pope Benedict XVI's encyclical *On Christian Hope* (*Spe Salvi*).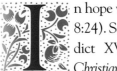

Pope Benedict knows the immense human suffering within the world. He recognizes that while much of this suffering is caused by natural calamities, more is caused by the sinful, evil deeds of men and women: for example, the Holocaust; war and terrorism; trafficking; societal and economic injustice. These evils give rise to the question: Is human life, with its history of horrendous suffering, hopeless?

For Pope Benedict, this crisis of hope is compounded within the secular culture of disbelief. He perceives that all men and women today both desperately need hope and search for a reason for hope. He is convinced that true authentic hope is found in the Gospel of Jesus Christ. He points out in his encyclical that St. Paul told the Ephesians that, before they came to faith in Jesus, they were "without hope and without God in the world" (Eph 2:12).

Why is Jesus the source of the hope? Through his death on the Cross, Jesus attends to the heart of human hopelessness—sin and evil, and the suffering they cause. Through his Resurrection, he holds out to every human person the hope of a divine transformation through faith and the power of the indwelling Holy Spirit. In Christ, human beings are offered a new way of life in this world, one that finds glorious completion in heaven.

Pope Benedict recognizes that no human means can redress adequately the heinous wrongs within our human history, nor are there human means to bring forth justice. "No one and nothing can answer for centuries of suffering" (no. 42), the Pope says in *On Christian Hope*. But he assures us that with the coming of Jesus in glory "there is a resurrection of the flesh. There is justice. There is an 'undoing' of past suffering, a reparation that sets things aright" (no. 43). Hope ensures that every tear will be wiped away. ∎

The Pope visits a tent camp in Onna, L'Aquila, Italy, April 28, 2009. Here, he comforts a woman who survived the April 6 earthquake.

Following: Pope Benedict XVI waves to the crowd after the Papal Mass at Nationals Park, April 17, 2008.

RESOURCES

The Life and Ministry of Pope Benedict XVI

Joseph A. Ratzinger

April 16, 1927

Joseph Alois Ratzinger is born in Marktl am Inn, Bavaria, Germany, and is baptized on the same day, Holy Saturday.

1939

Enters the minor seminary in Traunstein.

1941

Turns 14 and, as required by law at the time, joins the Hitler Youth.

1943

At age 16, Joseph Ratzinger and the rest of his seminary class are drafted into the German anti-aircraft corps. A year later he is drafted into the Austrian Legion and undergoes basic training in the German infantry.

1945

In the spring, Joseph Ratzinger deserts the army and returns home to Traunstein. He is briefly held by American forces in a prisoner of war camp. After he is released, he and his brother Georg reenter the seminary.

1946-1951

Studies philosophy and theology at the Higher School of Philosophy and Theology of Freising and the Herzogliches Georgianum, a theological institute associated with the University of Munich.

June 29, 1951

Joseph Ratzinger and brother Georg are ordained priests by Cardinal Michael von Faulhaber of Munich.

1952

Begins teaching at the Higher School of Freising.

1953

In July, Father Ratzinger receives his doctorate in theology from the University of Munich. The title of his thesis is *People and House of God in St. Augustine's Doctrine of the Church*.

1957

Qualifies for university teaching. Writes his dissertation on *The Theology of History in St. Bonaventure*.

1959

Begins lecturing as a full-time professor of fundamental theology at the University of Bonn. On August 23, his father dies.

1962-1965

Participates in all four sessions of the Second Vatican Council as chief theological advisor to Cardinal Joseph Frings of Cologne, Germany.

1963

Starts teaching at the University of Münster. On December 16, his mother dies.

1966

Accepts a chair in dogmatic theology at the University of Tübingen.

1969

A wave of student uprisings driven, in large part, by Marxist ideologies and the rejection of traditional religion disillusions Father Ratzinger. He leaves Tübingen and returns to Bavaria to teach at the University of Regensburg.

1972

Founds, together with Hans Urs von Balthasar, Henri de Lubac and other renowned theologians, the quarterly journal of Catholic theology *Communio*.

March 25, 1977

Is appointed Archbishop of Munich and Freising by Pope Paul VI.

May 28, 1977

Is ordained bishop. Father Ratzinger is the first diocesan priest in 80 years to take on the pastoral governance of the Bavarian archdiocese. Chooses as his episcopal motto "Cooperators of the Truth."

June 27, 1977

Is elevated to the College of Cardinals by Pope Paul VI. He is assigned to the Church of Santa Maria Consolatrice al Tiburtino.

August 25-26, 1978

Takes part in the conclave that elects Pope John Paul I.

October 15-16, 1978

Takes part in the conclave that elects Pope John Paul II.

1980

Pope John Paul II asks him to lead the Congregation for Catholic Education at the Vatican. He declines.

November 25, 1981

Pope John Paul II names Cardinal Ratzinger prefect of the Congregation for the Doctrine of Faith, president of the Pontifical Biblical Commission, and president of the International Theological Commission.

1984

Receives an honorary doctorate from the College of St. Thomas in St. Paul, Minn.

1986

Receives an honorary doctorate from the Catholic University of Lima, Peru.

1987

Receives an honorary doctorate from the Catholic University of Eichstätt, Germany.

1988

Receives an honorary doctorate from the Catholic University of Lublin, Poland.

April 5, 1993

Is elevated by Pope John Paul II to the Order of Bishops within the College of Cardinals, assigning to him the suburbicarian (titulary) see of Velletri-Segni.

1986-1992

Serves as president of the Preparatory Commission for the *Catechism of the Catholic Church*.

1998

Receives an honorary doctorate from the University of Navarre, Spain.

November 6, 1998

Pope John Paul II approves of the election of Cardinal Ratzinger as the vice dean of the College of Cardinals.

1999

Receives an honorary doctorate from the LUMSA (Libera Università Maria Santissima Assunta) of Rome.

2000

Receives an honorary doctorate from the Faculty of Theology of the University of Wroclaw in Poland.

November 13, 2000

Is named an honorary academic of the Pontifical Academy of Sciences.

November 30, 2002

Pope John Paul II approves of the election of Cardinal Ratzinger as the dean of the College of Cardinals and gives him the title of Cardinal-Bishop of Ostia.

April 2005

Upon the death of Pope John Paul II, he resigns as prefect of the Congregation for the Doctrine of Faith and participates in the conclave to elect the next pope (April 18-19).

Life and Ministry After Election as Pope[1]

This list does not include many regular activities in the life of Pope Benedict XVI, such as multiple *ad limina* visits by bishops from all over the world, internal addresses to pontifical councils and academies, or ceremonies to receive and accept credentials of ambassadors to the Vatican from throughout the world. Only a few of his apostolic trips inside Italy are highlighted.

2005

April 19, 2005
Is elected as the 265th pope. Adopts the name of Benedict XVI, in honor of St. Benedict, the founder of Western monasticism, and of Benedict XV, pope during World War I and a promoter of peace.

April 22, 2005
Meets with all the cardinals present in Rome, including those over age 80 who did not vote in the conclave.

April 24, 2005
Benedict XVI is formally inaugurated as pope.

April 25, 2005
Meets with leaders of non-Catholic churches and religions including Christians, Buddhists and Muslims.

Makes his first official visit into the city of Rome, to visit the Basilica of St. Paul Outside the Walls.

April 28, 2005
Receives a delegation of officers from the Latin American Bishops' Council, who present the new Pope with a proposal for the Fifth General Conference of Latin American Bishops.

April 30, 2005
Approves the election of Cardinal Angelo Sodano, Vatican secretary of state, as the new dean of the College of Cardinals.

May 3, 2005
Meets with Italian President Carlo Azeglio Ciampi, the first head of state to have a private audience with Pope Benedict XVI.

May 7, 2005
As Bishop of Rome, Pope Benedict XVI takes possession of the Basilica of St. John Lateran, the diocesan cathedral.

May 12, 2005
Has first meeting with the diplomatic corps accredited to the Holy See.

May 13, 2005
Names Archbishop William J. Levada of San Francisco prefect of the Vatican Congregation for the Doctrine of the Faith, the post Pope Benedict occupied before being elected pope.

Waives the normal five-year waiting period for the introduction of the sainthood cause of Pope John Paul II.

May 29, 2005
Makes *first Italian journey* and celebration of Mass outside Rome as Pope Benedict XVI, to Bari.

May 30, 2005
During a meeting of the Italian bishops' general assembly, Benedict XVI speaks publicly in support of the bishops' campaign against Italy's June 12-13 referendum on artificial reproduction and human embryonic research.

---

1 Sources: Vatican Web site, Catholic News Service and Our Sunday Visitor's *Catholic Almanac.*

June 9, 2005
Meets at the Vatican with 25 leaders of the world's major Jewish organizations.

June 16, 2005
Welcomes to the Vatican a delegation of the World Council of Churches.

June 24, 2005
Makes *first official state visit to Italy*. Visits Italian President Azeglio Ciampi at Rome's presidential residence, the Quirinal Palace.

June 28, 2005
Releases the *Compendium of the Catechism of the Catholic Church*.

June 29, 2005
On the Feast of Sts. Peter and Paul, presides over *pallium* ceremony in St. Peter's Basilica to welcome 32 new archbishops from around the world, including four from the United States: Wilton D. Gregory of Atlanta, José H. Gomez of San Antonio, Joseph A. Fiorenza of Galveston-Houston, and Joseph F. Naumann of Kansas City, Kansas.

Receives delegation representing Ecumenical Orthodox Patriarch Bartholomew of Constantinople to resume Catholic-Orthodox dialogue.

July 7, 2005
Through Israel's ambassador to the Holy See, Oded Ben-Hur, Prime Minister Ariel Sharon extends an invitation for him to visit Israel.

August 18-21, 2005
Makes *first foreign apostolic journey* and homecoming as Pope. Travels to Cologne, Germany, for World Youth Day. Meets with German president Horst Koehler.

August 29, 2005
Meets with Bishop Bernard Fellay, superior general of the Society of St. Pius X, a schismatic priestly society founded by Archbishop Marcel Lefebvre after he broke with Rome.

September 1, 2005
Appeals to Iraqi Christians and Muslims to condemn jointly the violence in their country after a tragedy a few days earlier left more than 900 Shiite pilgrims dead.

September 12, 2005
Receives King Abdullah II of Jordan and Queen Rania.

September 15, 2005
Meets with Shlomo Moshe Amar and Yona Metzger, Israel's two chief rabbis, who issue an invitation for him to visit Jerusalem.

September 24, 2005
Meets with German theologian Father Hans Küng in Castel Gandolfo.

October 2-23, 2005
Presides over the *Synod of Bishops on the Eucharist* at the Vatican. It is the largest synod to date with 256 synod fathers from 118 nations participating.

October 7, 2005
After seeing laws supporting same-sex marriages pass in Spain, as well as attempts to legalize euthanasia for terminally ill patients in England, Pope Benedict XVI sends a message to the Plenary Assembly of the Council of European Bishops' Conferences, encouraging them to "continue to preach the Gospel of hope to all" in the midst of a culture characterized by secularism.

October 17, 2005
Sends a letter to the president of the Italian Senate calling for a "positive secularity in the world," one that would omit hostility between religion and state.

Pope Benedict's public appearances are drawing record crowds to the Vatican. More than 1 million people have attended the Pope's weekly general audience or his Sunday blessings between his election in April and October. The number rises to close to 3 million by the end of December.

October 23, 2005

Canonizes the first saints of his pontificate, from Italy, Poland and Chile, marking also the closing of the Synod of Bishops on the Eucharist and World Mission Sunday.

November 10, 2005

Meets privately with Iraqi President Jalal Talabani and urges him to support the country's minority Christian population. It marks the *first time an Iraqi president visits Italy and the Vatican.*

November 12, 2005

Receives credentials of new U.S. ambassador to the Vatican, Francis Rooney.

November 19, 2005

Turns authority over the two Franciscan basilicas in Assisi to the local bishop and issues new norms.

November 20, 2005

Receives Italian Prime Minister Silvio Berlusconi.

December 3, 2005

Meets with Palestinian Prime Minister Mahmoud Abbas.

December 8, 2005

Authorizes special plenary indulgences to mark the 40th anniversary of the Second Vatican Council.

December 15, 2005

Meets with committee of the international Catholic-Orthodox dialogue.

December 18, 2005

Appoints Archbishop Pietro Sambi as apostolic nuncio to the United States.

December 25, 2005

Issues *Deus Caritas Est* (*God Is Love*), the first encyclical letter of his pontificate.

✠ 2006

February 22, 2006

Announces the creation of 15 new cardinals from 11 countries, including two from the United States: Archbishops William J. Levada, prefect of the Congregation for the Doctrine of Faith, and Seán P. O'Malley of Boston. The cardinals are officially installed at a special consistory on March 24.

March 13, 2006

Holds private meeting with Egyptian President Hosni Mubarak.

March 22, 2006

The Pontifical Council for Promoting Christian Unity issues a statement regarding Pope Benedict XVI's decision to cease using the title "Patriarch of the West."

May 11, 2006

Meets with Venezuelan President Hugo Chávez.

May 19, 2006

Decrees that Father Marcial Maciel Degollado, founder of the Legionaries of Christ, should no longer exercise his priestly ministry in public.

May 25-28, 2006

Makes *second foreign apostolic journey,* a four-day visit to Poland. The trip includes a meeting with President Lech Kaczynsky and visits to Nazi death camps at Auschwitz and Birkenau.

June 3, 2006

Meets with British Prime Minister Tony Blair.

June 26, 2006

Receives Filipino President Gloria Macapagal-Arroyo, who presents the Holy Father with a copy of a recent law outlawing the death penalty in the Philippines.

July 2, 2006

Authorizes the opening of the Vatican archives for the pontificate of Pope Pius XI, covering the years 1922-1936.

July 3, 2006

Sends a message to the people of Poznan, Poland, on the occasion of the 50th anniversary of the first anti-Stalinist insurgency in a Soviet bloc country.

July 8-9, 2006

Makes *third foreign apostolic journey*, a visit to Valencia, Spain, for the fifth World Meeting of Families.

July 30, 2006

At his midday Angelus address, begs the world leaders to arrange for a Middle East ceasefire, after Israeli missiles leave many victims in a Lebanon village.

August 11, 2006

Executions of three Catholics in Indonesia are halted after an appeal by Benedict XVI to Indonesian officials.

September 9-14, 2006

Makes *fourth foreign apostolic journey*, a visit to Munich, Altötting and Regensburg, Germany.

September 12, 2006

Muslim leaders take offense at some of the Pope's comments in his address to academics in the University of Regensburg in Bavaria.

September 14, 2006

A statement is issued explaining the context and purpose of a quotation from medieval times.

September 19, 2006

Pope Benedict's message to clarify his words on Islam is published in Arabic on the front page of *L'Osservatore Romano*.

October 13, 2006

Receives the Dalai Lama, Tenzin Gyatso, in private audience.

November 28–December 1, 2006

Makes *fifth foreign apostolic journey*, a four-day visit to Turkey. Celebrates Mass in Ephesus. Visits with Ecumenical Orthodox Patriarch Bartholomew I in Istanbul and visits the Blue Mosque.

December 11, 2006

It is announced that Rome's four patriarchal basilicas will henceforth be referred to as "papal" basilicas.

December 13, 2006

Receives Israeli Prime Minister Ehud Olmert.

December 14, 2006

Meets with Orthodox Archbishop Christodoulos of Athens and All Greece. Together, in this historic meeting, they sign a joint declaration reaffirming the collaboration of Orthodox and Catholics.

2007

January 7, 2007

Accepts resignation of Warsaw's Archbishop Stanislaw Wielgus, after he acknowledges collaborating with Poland's communist secret police years earlier.

January 24, 2007

Receives, as a gift to the Holy See, the Bodmer Papyrus (P75), an ancient manuscript of the Gospels (dated between AD 175-225), previously owned by the Frank Hanna family of the United States and preserved in the library of the Bodmer Foundation in Switzerland.

January 25, 2007

Welcomes Vietnamese Prime Minister Nguyen Tan Dung. Becomes the first Pope to receive a communist Vietnamese leader in an audience. In March, an announcement is made about the Vietnamese government's steps towards establishing diplomatic relations with the Holy See.

March 13, 2007

Announces the publication of *Sacramentum Caritatis* (*The Sacrament of Charity*), an apostolic exhortation that gathers the conclusions of the 2005 Synod of Bishops on the Eucharist and encourages the wider use of Latin in international celebrations and Masses.

Receives Russian President Vladimir Putin in private audience.

March 23, 2007
Receives Irish President Mary McAleese in audience.

April 18, 2007
Publishes *first book* as Pope Benedict XVI. The first volume, *Jesus of Nazareth*, sells more than 50,000 copies on a single day in Italy.

Receives the United Nations Secretary-General Ban Ki-Moon, who invites him to visit the United Nations.

April 24, 2007
Welcomes to the Vatican with head-of-state honors Palestinian President Mahmoud Abbas, and meets with him in private audience.

April 27, 2007
Accepts invitation to visit the United Nations, although no particular date is set.

May 9-13, 2007
Makes *sixth foreign apostolic journey*, a four-day visit to Brazil, for the opening of the Fifth General Conference of the Latin American and Caribbean Bishops.

June 4, 2007
Receives in audience Mexican President Felipe Calderón.

June 6, 2007
A mentally disabled man of German nationality jumps over the barricades at St. Peter's Square and holds on to the "popemobile" for a few seconds. Pope Benedict XVI is not hurt.

June 10, 2007
Receives in audience the president of the United States, George W. Bush.

June 16, 2007
Welcomes to the Vatican Orthodox Archbishop Chrysostomos II of Cyprus, head of the Orthodox Church in Cyprus. After a five-hour meeting, they sign a joint declaration of ecumenical commitment.

✠ June 21, 2007
Receives in audience the patriarch of the Assyrian Church of the East, Mar Dinkha IV, who conveys to the Holy Father the difficult situation of the Assyrian Christian faithful, particularly those in Iraq.

June 26, 2007
Reinstitutes the rule that a two-thirds majority be required always to elect a pope.

June 30, 2007
Issues an open letter to mainland Chinese Catholics calling for unity between the registered and unregistered communities.

July 8, 2007
Authorizes expanded use of the Tridentine rite for Mass in his apostolic letter *Summorum Pontificum*.

July 10, 2007
Approves the release by the Congregation for the Doctrine of the Faith of a document on *Certain Aspects of the Doctrine on the Church*.

August 12, 2007
Appeals to the international community to come to the aid of millions affected by severe flooding in several countries of south Asia.

September 5, 2007
Meets in private audience with Syria's Vice-President Farouk al-Sharaa to discuss the exodus of Christian and other refugees from Iraq into Syria.

September 6, 2007
Meets with Israeli President Shimon Peres.

September 7, 2007
Sends written message to environmental and religious leaders who are meeting in Greenland and makes a call to industrialized nations to "share clean technologies" with developing nations.

September 7-9, 2007
Makes *seventh foreign apostolic journey*, a three-day visit to Austria.

September 11, 2007

Accepts the resignation of Zimbabwean Archbishop Pius Ncube of Bulawayo amid his criticism of the country's dictatorial president and a sexual allegation brought against him.

September 30, 2007

Appeals for a peaceful resolution to the crisis in Myanmar (Burma).

October 8, 2007

Welcomes to the Vatican President Ronald S. Lauder and new leaders of the World Jewish Congress.

October 9, 2007

Names two Nobel laureates, Taiwanese professor Yuan Tseh Lee and German professor Klaus von Klitzing, as members of the Pontifical Academy of Sciences.

October 11, 2007

More than 100 senior Muslim leaders and scholars from around the world send a letter to Pope Benedict XVI and other Christian leaders proposing theological similarities as a basis for peace and understanding.

October 14, 2007

Appeals for the release of two Catholic priests kidnapped in Iraq on October 13.

October 25, 2007

Meets with Zeljko Komsic, a Catholic Croat and president of Bosnia-Herzegovina. After the meeting Komsic formally exchanges documents marking ratification of a concordat, with Vatican officials designed to guarantee religious rights and freedoms for the Catholic Church in Bosnia-Herzegovina.

October 28, 2007

The *beatification of 498 martyrs of the 1936-1939 Spanish Civil War* at St. Peter's Square sets a new record for beatifications in one day. In spite of the tensions created in Spain by the decision, the Pope says he hopes the martyrs' words and gestures of forgiveness toward their persecutors will lead Christians to work tirelessly for mercy, reconciliation and peaceful coexistence.

✠ **November 4, 2007**

At his Angelus address, calls for a peaceful solution to mounting tensions between Turkey and northern Iraq and expresses concern for the Kurdish people in northern Iraq.

November 6, 2007

For the first time the Pope meets with a reigning Saudi Arabian monarch, King Abdullah Aziz. Saudi Arabia and the Vatican do not have formal diplomatic ties.

November 24, 2007

Holds *second consistory* of his pontificate where he officially inducts 23 new cardinals, including two from the United States: Archbishop John P. Foley, Pro-Grand Master of the Equestrian Order of the Holy Sepulcher in Jerusalem, and Archbishop Daniel N. DiNardo of Galveston-Houston, first cardinal from the southern part of the United States.

November 29, 2007

Responds to a letter from 138 Muslim scholars by inviting a group of them to meet with him and with the Pontifical Council for Interreligious Dialogue.

November 30, 2007

Releases *Spe Salvi* (*On Christian Hope*), the *second encyclical letter* of his pontificate.

December 2, 2007

In his first visit as Pope Benedict XVI to a Rome hospital, urges hospitals and health care workers to welcome patients with love and safeguard their dignity.

December 5, 2007

Authorizes a special plenary indulgence to mark the 150th anniversary of Mary's appearance to St. Bernadette Soubirous near Lourdes, France.

December 7, 2007

Meets in private with Orthodox Metropolitan Kirill of Smolensk and Kaliningrad, head of the Moscow Patriarchate's office for external relations.

December 12, 2007
An international group of Muslim scholars accepts an invitation from Pope Benedict XVI for a major dialogue session at the Vatican.

December 18, 2007
Establishes a commission to study newly discovered archival material about the papacy of Pope Pius XII.

December 20, 2007
Welcomes to the Vatican French President Nicolas Sarkozy.

December 27, 2007
Condemns the assassination at an election rally of former Pakistan Prime Minister Benazir Bhutto.

2008

January 5, 2008
Appeals for an immediate end to ethnic violence in Kenya.

January 6, 2008
On the Feast of the Epiphany, a German solar company gives, as a gift to the Pope, an electricity-generating solar rooftop for the Vatican's Paul VI Audience Hall. Installation of the solar panels took place in the fall of 2008.

January 10, 2008
Condemns the latest attacks on Christian churches in Iraq and urges a return to peaceful coexistence among the country's diverse groups.

Names renown hydrologist Ignacio Rodriguez-Iturbe, a Venezuelan-born U.S. citizen, and professor at Princeton University to the Pontifical Academy of Sciences.

January 15, 2008
Cancels his scheduled January 17 visit to Rome's public University of La Sapienzia, following a letter of protest signed by 67 professors and threats of student demonstrations.

January 20, 2008
Tens of thousands of Romans, among them many university students, fill St. Peter's Square in a show of support for Pope Benedict XVI, three days after he canceled a university appearance because of protests.

January 25, 2008
Presides over an evening prayer service at the Vatican concluding the Week of Prayer for Christian Unity. He is joined by representatives of the Protestant, Anglican, Orthodox and Oriental Orthodox churches. The 2008 observance marked the 100th anniversary of the week of prayer, which was begun in New York.

January 30, 2008
Reorganizes Eastern rite Catholic Church in Slovakia in recognition of the growth and stability of the Church in what was once communist Czechoslovakia.

January 31, 2008
Appoints renowned Japanese molecular biologist Takashi Gojobori to the Pontifical Academy of Sciences.

February 5, 2008
Reformulates the Tridentine rite's Good Friday prayer for Jews.

February 13, 2008
Announces he will dispense with the five-year waiting period required by canon law to open the cause of beatification for Sister Lucia, one of the three Fatima visionaries.

Accepts letters of credence and receives Mary Ann Glendon as new U.S. ambassador to the Holy See. Glendon will remain in the post until January 19, 2009.

March 1-2, 2008
Appeals for the release of Paulos Faraj Rahho, Chaldean Archbishop of Mosul, Iraq.

March 6, 2008
Receives in audience the Orthodox Patriarch Bartholomew I of Constantinople.

March 22, 2008

At a Holy Saturday liturgy in St. Peter's Basilica, baptizes Muslim-born journalist Magdi Allam.

April 15-20, 2008

Makes *eighth foreign apostolic journey*, to the United States and the United Nations (Washington and New York City). For the first time, Pope Benedict meets personally with victims of sexual abuse by clergy, at the Vatican embassy in Washington.

April 30, 2008

Receives representatives of the Pontifical Council for Interreligious Dialogue and the Tehran-based Center for Interreligious Dialogue of the Islamic Culture and Relations Organization who are studying together faith and reason in their respective faiths.

May 5, 2008

Receives in audience the Anglican Archbishop Rowan Williams of Canterbury.

May 9, 2008

On the 50th anniversary of the creation of the Pontifical Commission for Latin America, receives a delegation of the Council of Latin American Bishops' Conferences (CELAM).

The Vatican Web site launches an edition in the Church's official language—Latin.

June 13, 2008

Receives in audience U.S. President George W. Bush.

June 28-29, 2008

Opens the *Jubilee Year of St. Paul* to celebrate the 2,000th anniversary of the birth of St. Paul. The ecumenical Patriarch of Constantinople Bartholomew I participates in both the vespers service on Saturday and Mass the next day. In a sign of Christian unity, both the Pope and the patriarch pronounce the homily; together they recite the profession of faith and impart the blessing.

July 12-21, 2008

Makes *ninth foreign apostolic journey*, a visit to Australia for the 23rd World Youth Day celebrations.

✠ **July 25, 2008**

Meets with Iraqi Prime Minister Nouri al-Malaki, discussing the worsening situation for Christians in Iraq.

August 10, 2008

Makes appeal for the immediate cessation of hostilities in South Ossetia, Georgia, after Russia launches military operations against the former Soviet province.

September 12-15, 2008

Makes *tenth foreign trip*, an apostolic journey to France (Paris and Lourdes).

September 22, 2008

Urges world leaders, who will soon join the UN General Assembly to evaluate progress on the Millennium Development Goals, to tackle global poverty "with courage."

October 6-15, 2008

Convenes the *World Synod of Bishops on the Word of God in the Life and Mission of the Church.*

October 30, 2008

Meets with the International Jewish Committee on Interreligious Consultations, who represent the main branches of Judaism and the world's largest Jewish organizations.

October 31, 3008

Meets in private audience with Lebanese President Michel Sleiman.

November 6, 2008

Meets with the members of the newly created Catholic-Muslim Forum, which holds its first meeting November 4-6, 2008, at the Vatican.

November 9, 2008

Marks the 70th anniversary of Kristallnacht (Night of the Broken Glass) by asking Catholics to pray for the Jewish victims of the Holocaust and condemning all forms of anti-Semitism.

November 13, 2008

Welcomes President Luiz Inacio Lula da Silva of Brazil to the Vatican for the signing ceremony of an agreement on the Catholic Church's legal status and rights in Brazil.

2009

January 23, 2009

The Vatican launches a video channel on You-Tube to feature news coverage of Pope Benedict XVI and major Vatican events in an effort to "be present wherever people are."

January 26, 2009

The Vatican formally announces that Pope Benedict XVI has lifted the excommunication against four traditionalist bishops of the Society of St. Pius X.

January 28, 2009

Condemns all ignorance, denial and downplaying of the "brutal slaughter of millions of Jewish people during the Holocaust," in the wake of controversial comments by British-born Bishop Richard Williamson of the traditionalist Society of St. Pius X, whose excommunication was lifted just a few days earlier.

February 18, 2009

Meets with U.S. House Speaker Nancy Pelosi (D-Calif.) at the Vatican and stresses to her the Church's pro-life teaching.

February 19, 2009

Receives at the Vatican British Prime Minister Gordon Brown.

March 12, 2009

In a letter to the world's bishops, expresses regret that his lifting of the excommunications of four bishops of the Society of St. Pius X gave rise to a storm of protests and bitterness.

Meets representatives of the Chief Rabbinate of Israel and pledges continued efforts to improve Catholic-Jewish relations.

March 17-23, 2009

Makes *eleventh foreign apostolic journey*, a trip to Africa: Cameroon and Angola.

✠ April 18, 2009

Grants the Congregation for Clergy new powers to dismiss from the priesthood and release from the obligation of celibacy priests who are living with women, who have abandoned their ministry for more than five years or who have engaged in seriously scandalous behavior.

April 29, 2009

Meets a delegation of Canada's native peoples and expresses his sorrow for the suffering of Canadian indigenous children over decades in church-run residential schools.

May 8-15, 2009

Makes *twelfth foreign apostolic journey*, a trip to the Holy Land (Jordan, Israel and the Palestinian territories).

May 24, 2009

Prays for peace and honors fallen World War II soldiers in a visit to Cassino and Monte Cassino Abbey, founded by St. Benedict.

May 26, 2009

Accepts the resignation of Archbishop Paulin Pomodimo of Bangui, Zambia, following an investigation into priests of his diocese who are said to live openly with women and the children they have fathered.

June 1, 2009

Meets with Ukrainian President Viktor Yushchenko at the Vatican. They discuss ongoing government efforts to return church properties confiscated by the government when Ukraine was under Soviet rule.

June 8, 2009

Meets with Ireland's Cardinal Sean Brady of Armagh and Archbishop Diarmuid Martin of Dublin on the results of the Ryan Report published May 20, which unveiled the abuse of children in institutions run by the Catholic Church. The Pope was said to be visibly upset from hearing about "how the children had suffered from the very opposite of an expression of the love of God."

June 16, 2009

Meets with leaders of the Austrian church to discuss local problems, including repeated public calls by a group of lay Catholics for the Church to drop the celibacy requirement because of a shortage of priests and the uproar after Pope Benedict's decision in February, later revoked, to name controversial Msgr. Gerhard Wagner to be auxiliary bishop for the Diocese of Linz.

June 19, 2009

Inaugurates the *Year for Priests* on the Solemnity of the Most Sacred Heart of Jesus.

June 29, 2009

Five new U.S. archbishops—Archbishop Timothy M. Dolan of New York, Archbishop Gregory M. Aymond of New Orleans, Archbishop Allen H. Vigneron of Detroit, Archbishop George J. Lucas of Omaha and Archbishop Robert J. Carlson of St. Louis—receive the *pallium* from Pope Benedict XVI during a special Mass in St. Peter's Basilica. In total, 34 archbishops from 20 countries received the white, narrow circular woolen band that signals their communion with the successor of Peter.

July 7, 2009

Caritas in Veritate (*Charity in Truth*), Pope Benedict's third encyclical letter, is released.

July 10, 2009

Receives in audience U.S. President Barack Obama, after the president's participation at the G-8 summit in L'Aquila, Italy.

July 17, 2009

Falls during his vacation at the Italian Alps and fractures his right wrist. Undergoes surgery and wears a cast for the next several weeks.

July 28, 2009

Laicizes a Franciscan priest who served as the spiritual adviser to the Marian visionaries in Medjugorje, Bosnia-Herzegovina.

July 30, 2009

Announcement that the Pope's home in Bavaria, Germany, will become a solar-power generator. Income from this project will go towards skills building and job training for underprivileged youth.

August 3, 2009

Expresses his sadness at the death of former Philippine President Corazon Aquino and praises her commitment to freedom and justice for Filipinos.

Deplores the killing of eight Christians in Pakistan by a Muslim mob and urges the minority Christian community not to be deterred by the attack.

August 21, 2009

Doctors remove cast from Pope Benedict's right wrist. Healing process went perfectly.

September 16, 2009

Visits and officially inaugurates the Vatican Observatory's new headquarters in Castel Gandolfo.

September 18, 2009

Meets with Archbishop Hilarion of the Moscow Patriarchate. The meeting shows significant improvement in relations with the Russian Orthodox Church.

Announces a Synod of Bishops for the Middle East to be held in October 2010 to address the hardships that the Christian populations of that region face.

September 26-28, 2009

Apostolic journey to the Czech Republic: Prague, Brno and Stara Boleslav.

September 30, 2009

Names Cardinal Seán P. O'Malley of Boston and five other U.S. Catholics to positions on the Pontifical Council for the Family. Cardinal O'Malley will serve on the *presiding committee* of the council.

October 2, 2009

Welcomes Professor Miguel Diaz as the new U.S. ambassador to the Vatican.

Names J. Russell Hittinger, a U.S. professor of Catholic studies at the University of Tulsa, Okla., as a member of the Pontifical Academy of Social Sciences.

October 4-25, 2009

Presides over second *Special Assembly for Africa* of the Synod of Bishops at the Vatican.

October 8, 2009

Meets with Palestinian President Mahmoud Abbas in a private audience at the Vatican.

October 10, 2009

Names two prominent U.S. geneticists, Francis S. Collins and Edward M. De Robertis, to the Pontifical Academy of Sciences.

✠ October 11, 2009

Canonizes five new saints, including Father Damien de Veuster, the 19th-century Belgian missionary who ministered to people with leprosy in Hawaii.

October 15, 2009

Announces the start of conversations with the breakaway Society of St. Pius X.

October 16, 2009

In a written message to the director-general of the UN Food and Agriculture Organization, Jacques Diouf, says that "determined and effective choices" must be made in investing in agriculture in the developing world.

The Holy Father speaks on the telephone in the papal office, Nov. 2007.

October 23, 2009

Appoints U.S. Archbishop Raymond L. Burke, head of the Vatican's highest tribunal, to serve also in the Congregation for Bishops.

October 24, 2009

Names African Cardinal Peter Turkson as head of the Pontifical Council for Justice and Peace.

November 9, 2009

Publishes *Anglicanorum Coetibus*, which will allow former Anglicans to come into full communion with the Catholic Church while maintaining some of their Anglican traditions.

November 16, 2009

Addresses the UN World Summit on Food Security during the opening session of a three-day conference in Rome.

November 21, 2009

Meets more than 250 artists from around the world under the frescoes of the Sistine Chapel to highlight the Church's traditional special relationship with the arts.

Meets privately with Anglican Archbishop Rowan Williams of Canterbury at the Vatican to discuss recent events affecting relations between the Catholic Church and Anglican Communion.

2010

January 17, 2010

Visits Rome's main synagogue for the first time as Pope.

January 25, 2010

Participates in the annual prayer service for Christian unity at the Basilica of St. Paul Outside the Walls with Leaders of Orthodox, Anglican and Protestant communities in Rome.

February 15-16, 2010

Meets with 24 bishops of Ireland on the local church's handling of priestly sex abuse cases and the wounds left by the scandal. Calls sexual abuse of children a "heinous crime" and a "sin" and urges Irish bishops to act courageously to repair their failures to deal properly with such cases.

March 3, 2010

Vatican announces Pope Benedict will travel November 6-7 to Spain (Barcelona and Santiago de Compostela).

March 12, 2010

Meets with Archbishop Robert Zollitsch of Freiburg, head of the German bishops' conference, on sexual abuse scandals in Catholic schools in Germany and encourages him to move ahead "with decision and courage" in investigating old cases and preventing new ones.

March 20, 2010

In his *Letter to Irish Catholics* apologizes to victims of sexual abuse by priests and promises new actions to heal the wounds of the scandal. Says bishops have made serious mistakes in responding to allegations of sexual abuse and encourages them to implement new church norms against abuse and cooperate with civil authorities.

April 1, 2010

Earmarks the Holy Thursday collection at St. John Lateran, Rome's cathedral, for the rebuilding of Haiti's major seminary in Port-au-Prince.

April 17-18, 2010

Apostolic journey to Malta: On April 18, meets privately in Rabat with eight men who had been abused as children by priests.

May 11-14

Apostolic journey to Portugal (Lisbon, Fatima and Porto). Presides over the annual ceremonies May 13 in Fatima.

KEY WRITINGS OF POPE BENEDICT XVI

The following summaries come from Origins, *the documentary service of Catholic News Service.*

ENCYCLICALS

God Is Love (*Deus Caritas Est*), December 25, 2005—Pope Benedict's first encyclical is "on Christian love." It explores divine love as it relates to human love and the meaning of "eros" and "agape," as well as the commandment to love one's neighbor. The Pope explores how different aspects of love cannot be cut off from one another. He discusses how the Eucharist unites love of God and love of others. He examines Catholic social teaching; the relationship of church and state in building a just social order; the independence of Christian charitable activity from "parties and ideologies"; humility in the face of "the immensity" of needs; and the necessity of prayer. Charity, the Pope says, is "an indispensable expression of [the church's] very being."

On Christian Hope (*Spe Salvi*), November 30, 2007—Pope Benedict's second encyclical focuses on hope and how it is rooted in knowing God. The encyclical addresses what the Pope calls a "crisis of Christian hope" in modern times. Pope Benedict warns that the modern world has replaced belief in eternal salvation with "faith in progress" and technology. The strong emphasis on reason and freedom today sometimes can go so far as to displace Christian hope, where redemption can be seen as possible through science and political programs, and where religious faith is relegated to the private sphere, the Pope says. By virtue of hope, the Pope explains, people can face even the most arduous present circumstances.

Charity in Truth (*Caritas in Veritate*), June 29, 2009—In his third encyclical, Pope Benedict explores the ethics of the global economy and urges businesses and governments to remember that the human person is the most important asset. He echoes concerns voiced by Pope Paul VI in his encyclical *Populorum Progressio* and speaks to a range of issues including human development, care for the environment and technology.

APOSTOLIC EXHORTATION

The Sacrament of Charity (*Sacramentum Caritatis*), February 22, 2007—In his post-synodal exhortation responding to the 2005 World Synod of Bishops on the Eucharist, Pope Benedict offers "some basic directions aimed at a renewed commitment to eucharistic enthusiasm and fervor in the church," and encourages "the Christian people to deepen their understanding of the relationship between the eucharistic mystery, the liturgical action and the new spiritual worship which derives from the Eucharist as the sacrament of charity" (no. 5).

MOTU PROPRIO

Summorum Pontificum, July 7, 2007—In the apostolic letter *Summorum Pontificum*, Pope Benedict XVI eases the way for more widespread use of the Tridentine Mass, calling the Roman Missal promulgated by Pope Paul VI in 1970 the ordinary expression of the law of prayer of the Catholic Church of the Latin rite, but saying that "nonetheless, the *Roman Missal* promulgated by St. Pius V and reissued by Blessed John XXIII is to be considered as an extraordinary expression of that same '*lex orandi*' (law of prayer) and must be given due honor for its venerable and ancient usage." Pope Benedict calls the two missals "two usages of the one Roman rite" and says that the use of both should in no way divide the church. The Pope writes that in parishes where there is a "stable group of faithful who adhere to the earlier liturgical tradition," pastors should provide a Tridentine Mass; the document allows parishioners to appeal to the bishop and even to the Vatican if they feel their needs are not met. The Pope also says that special parishes may be created within dioceses for celebration of the older form.

LETTERS

Letter to Chinese Catholics, May 27, 2007—Pope Benedict XVI sent a long letter to Chinese Catholics, establishing new guidelines for cooperation between clandestine Catholic communities and those who have registered with the Chinese government. The Pope criticizes the limits placed on the Church in China by the government and asks for more contact between church and state officials in order to resolve problems, saying that "the Holy See always remains open to negotiations, so necessary if the difficulties of the present time are to be overcome."

✠ Letter to Bishops on the Lifting of the Excommunication of Lefebvrite Bishops, March 10, 2009—Pope Benedict XVI expresses regret that his lifting of the excommunications of four traditionalist bishops gave rise to protest and bitterness, and he says he was particularly saddened at the reaction of some Catholics who were ready to "attack me with open hostility" and seemed willing to believe the Pope was changing direction on Catholic-Jewish relations. The Pope says the controversy over Bishop Richard Williamson's statements denying the extent of the Holocaust was "an unforeseen mishap"—one that could have been anticipated, however, by paying more attention to information easily available on the Internet. Pope Benedict says he learned the lesson "that in the future in the Holy See we will have to pay greater attention to that source of news." Pope Benedict says that for the Society of St. Pius X, full communion with the Church implies acceptance of the teachings of the Second Vatican Council. He adds that some defenders of Vatican II need to be reminded that being faithful to the Council also means being faithful to the Church's entire doctrinal history.

BOOK

Jesus of Nazareth, May 15, 2007 (Doubleday)—The first book published by Pope Benedict XVI explores the public ministry of Jesus as the first of a planned two-volume set. In the foreword, the Pope says the book is not an exercise of the Magisterium but an expression of his personal "search for the face of the Lord."

CONTRIBUTORS

Sister Janice Bader, director of the National Religious Retirement Office, is a member of the Sisters of Most Precious Blood of O'Fallon, Mo., and holds a master of business administration degree from Southern Illinois University. She has delivered speeches on topics related to religious orders and retirement, the vow of poverty, ministry subsidies and common goods.

John Carr, secretary of the Department of Justice, Peace and Human Development of the United States Conference of Catholic Bishops (USCCB), holds a bachelor's degree from the University of St. Thomas and an honorary doctor of law degree from Barry College. He was director of the White House Conference on Families in 1979-1980 and director of the National Committee for Full Employment in the late 1970s. He has written on Catholics and political responsibility, housing and mediating structures, and he often speaks on the mission and message of Catholic social teaching and the moral dimensions of key public issues.

Don Clemmer is assistant director of media relations for the United States Conference of Catholic Bishops, specializing in the Conference's outreach through social media such as Twitter, Facebook and the USCCB Media Blog. He is a graduate of the University of St. Francis in Fort Wayne, Ind., and has a background in print, broadcast and new media.

Stephen Colecchi is the director of the USCCB's Office of International Justice and Peace. He holds a bachelor's degree in philosophy and religious studies from Holy Cross College, a master of arts degree in religion from Yale University, and a doctor of ministry degree from St. Mary's Seminary and University. Among other honors, he has received the Bene Merenti Medal from Pope John Paul II. He has written numerous articles on Catholic social teaching, social justice, and political responsibility, and he authored a *Leader's Guide to "Sharing Catholic Social Teaching"* and *In the Footsteps of Jesus: Resource Manual on Catholic Social Teaching*, both published by the United States Conference of Catholic Bishops.

Father Allan Deck, a Jesuit priest of the California Province, is executive director of the USCCB's Secretariat of Cultural Diversity in the Church. He holds a doctorate in Latin American studies from St. Louis University and a doctor of sacred theology degree in missiology from the Pontifical Gregorian University in Rome. He has served as a parish priest and director of Hispanic ministry in the Diocese of Orange, California. He was a co-founder and first president of the Academy of Catholic Hispanic Theologians of the United States (ACHTUS) as well as of the National Catholic Council for Hispanic Ministry (NCCHM). In 1997, he founded the Loyola Institute for Spirituality in Orange and served as its executive director for 10 years. Father Deck has written or edited six books and is a frequent contributor to *America* magazine.

Richard Doerflinger is associate director of the USCCB's Secretariat of Pro-Life Activities. He holds a master of arts in divinity degree from the University of Chicago and has pursued doctoral studies at the University of Chicago and The Catholic University of America. He is an adjunct fellow in bioethics and public policy at the National Catholic Bioethics Center. He frequently writes and speaks on euthanasia, assisted suicide, embryo experimentation and reproductive technologies. He has been published in such periodicals as *National Catholic Bioethics Quarterly*, *Kennedy Institute of Ethics Journal*, *Hastings Center Report*, *Linacre Quarterly*, and *Duquesne Law Review*.

Virginia Loo Farris is a foreign policy advisor in the USCCB's Office of International Justice and Peace, covering Eurasia and human rights issues. As a foreign service officer at the U.S. State Department and the U.S. Information Agency, she specialized in public diplomacy, focusing primarily on East and Southeast Asia. She also worked in Africa, Latin America, South Asia and Washington. She was selected as a Congressional Fellow and as USIA advisor to the commander of the U.S. Pacific Command. She has a master of science degree in national security studies from the National Defense University, a master of arts degree in Chinese studies from the University of Michigan, and a bachelor of arts degree in social sciences from Michigan State University.

Sheila Garcia, associate director of the USCCB's Secretariat of Laity, Marriage, Family Life and Youth, holds a bachelor's degree from Ohio University and a master's degree in theology from the DeSales School of Theology. She has written and spoken on topics related to marriage, domestic violence and women, and she has written for such publications as *Liguorian*, *Spiritual Life*, and *Catholic Woman*.

Carol Glatz covers the Vatican and other church issues on the international front as a correspondent for the Catholic News Service (CNS) Rome bureau. She has been honored by the Catholic Press Association for her coverage. Prior to joining CNS, she worked at Vatican Radio covering Vatican and world news. Originally from the Albany, N.Y., area, she has lived in Italy since 1994. She holds a bachelor's degree, magna cum laude, in political science and philosophy from Allegheny College in Meadville, Pa.

Stephen Hilbert, of the USCCB's Office of International Justice and Peace, holds a bachelor's degree in Russian studies from Haverford College and a master's degree in international affairs–development studies from Columbia University. From 1977-1980, he was a Peace Corps volunteer in Gabon, in central Africa. From 1983-2007 he worked with Catholic Relief Services, including 19 years in Africa, two years in India and three years at CRS headquarters.

Father Richard Hilgartner, a priest of the Archdiocese of Baltimore, is associate director of the USCCB Secretariat of Divine Worshop. He holds a bachelor of science degree (business and finance) from Mount St. Mary's College (now University) in Emmitsburg, Md.; a master of divinity degree and bachelor of sacred theology degree from St. Mary's Seminary and University, Baltimore; and a licentiate of sacred theology from the Pontificio Ateneo Sant'Anselmo, Rome. In addition to his work at the USCCB's Secretariat of Divine Worship, he is also pursuing doctoral studies in liturgy at The Catholic University of America. Father Hilgartner has served in parish ministry and campus ministry and has taught theology and homiletics.

Teresa M. Kettelkamp, executive director of the USCCB's Secretariat of Child and Youth Protection, is a graduate of Quincy University, Quincy, Ill., where she obtained a degree in political science. She retired from the Illinois State Police (ISP) after a 29-year career in which she was the first female to attain the rank of colonel. She began her law enforcement career investigating white collar and public corruption cases. During her career, she was also responsible for the functional supervision of specially trained agents who conducted statewide investigations involving missing and/or sexually exploited children. At her retirement, she headed the ISP's Division of Forensic Services.

Father James Massa, executive director of the USCCB's Secretariat of Ecumenical and Interreligious Affairs, is a priest of the Diocese of Brooklyn. He completed his undergraduate work at Boston College and the University of Durham in England. He pursued studies in theology at Yale Divinity School and doctoral studies at Fordham University, where he wrote on the ecclesiology of Joseph Ratzinger, now Pope Benedict XVI. He has published articles and book reviews on topics related to Christology, Church and culture, and ecumenism and is a member of the North American Academy of Ecumenists, the National Association of Ecumenical Officers, the Society of Catholic Liturgy, and the Fellowship of Catholic Scholars. He frequently lectures on topics related to ecumenical and interreligious dialogue.

Sister Eileen McCann, CSJ, is a member of the Sisters of St. Joseph of Carondelet, Albany, NY Province. She has been involved in youth and young adult ministry for more than 25 years, serving on the parish, diocesan, and national levels, and is now the coordinator for youth and young adult ministry of the USCCB's Secretariat of Laity, Marriage, Family Life and Youth. In 2008, she received the National Catholic Youth Ministry Award from the National Federation for Catholic Youth Ministry.

Maria del Mar Muñoz-Visoso, assistant director of media relations for the United States Conference of Catholic Bishops, holds a bachelor of arts degree in communications with a major in journalism from Centro Escuela Universitaria San Pablo in Valencia, Spain, and a master of theological studies degree from the Madonna University in Livonia, Mich. She has 18 years of experience as an editor and journalist and 12 years of experience in Hispanic ministry, with emphasis on leadership development, training and organizing. She has worked in radio and the written press and was the founding editor of *El Pueblo Católico*, a Catholic Spanish-language diocesan newspaper. She co-founded and was executive director of Centro San Juan Diego, a pastoral institute and adult education center for Hispanics in Denver.

Helen Osman holds a degree in communications from Drury College in Springfield, Mo., and has served in church communications for more than 25 years, beginning at the *Catholic Spirit*, the newspaper of the Diocese of Austin, Texas. She was named *Catholic Spirit's* editor in 1990 and added responsibilities as diocesan communications director in 1995. She was named secretary of communications for the United States Conference of Catholic Bishops in August 2007. Mrs. Osman served three terms on the board of directors of the Catholic Press Association (CPA) of the United States and Canada and held CPA positions as secretary and president.

Marie Powell holds a bachelor of arts degree, magna cum laude, from the College of St. Mary, Omaha, Neb., and a master of arts degree from Georgetown University. She has been involved in K-12 education in Catholic schools as a parent, teacher, administrator, diocesan superintendent of schools, chair of a diocesan school board, and assistant secretary for parental advocacy for the United States Conference of Catholic Bishops. She is currently the executive director of the USCCB's Secretariat of Catholic Education.

Father Ronald Roberson, associate director of the USCCB's Secretariat of Ecumenical and Interreligious Affairs, is a Paulist Father and holds a doctorate in oriental ecclesiastical sciences from the Pontifical Oriental Institute, Rome. He has written extensively on ecumenism and Catholic-Orthodox relations in scholarly journals and frequently speaks on related topics. He is also a member of the international dialogue between the Catholic Church and the Oriental Orthodox Churches.

Kathy A. Saile is director of the USCCB's Office of Domestic Social Development. She holds a bachelor's degree in organizational communications from Ohio University and a master's degree in social work from Arizona State University. Previously, she directed the Office of Peace and Justice in the Diocese of Phoenix, served as a loaned executive to the social policy office at Catholic Charities USA, coordinated social justice and outreach ministries for the Franciscan Renewal Center in Scottsdale, Az., and was associate director of public policy for Lutheran Services in America. She is the author of a book on public policy and grassroots advocacy.

Msgr. Anthony F. Sherman is director of the USCCB's Secretariat of Divine Worship. He holds a doctorate in sacred theology from the University of Innsbruck, Austria. Most recently he wrote an article on the implementation of the RCIA that appeared in the award-winning book *Impact of the RCIA*, edited by Jerry Galipeau.

Father Andrew Small, director of the USCCB's Collection for the Church in Latin America, holds a doctorate in sacred theology from The Catholic University of America as well as law degrees from the University of Sheffield in England and Georgetown University Law Center, where he is currently an adjunct professor of law. He has spoken widely on the relationship between church teaching and globalization, having served for five years as the U.S. bishops' principal foreign policy advisor on international economic questions.

John Thavis, Catholic News Service's Rome Bureau chief, holds a bachelor's degree from St. John's University, Collegeville, Minn. He has worked in the Rome Bureau since 1983 and as bureau chief since 1996. He is a past president of the Vatican Journalists Association and has been honored by the Catholic Press Association for his coverage of the Vatican and international affairs. His other writings include a guide book on Rome. He has traveled with popes to more than 60 countries.

Father David Toups is a priest of the Diocese of St. Petersburg, Florida. He holds a licentiate in sacred theology from the Pontifical Gregorian University and a doctorate in sacred theology from the Pontifical University of St. Thomas Aquinas (the Angelicum) in Rome. He has served as a parish priest, a professor of theology and dean of students at the major seminary in Florida. In 2008, he published *Reclaiming Our Priestly Character* through the Institute of Priestly Formation at Creighton University. He was on the staff of the USCCB Secretariat of Clergy, Consecrated Life and Vocations from 2007 to 2010.

Sister Mary Ann Walsh, director of the USCCB's Office of Media Relations, is a member of the Northeast Community of the Sisters of Mercy of the Americas. She holds a master's degree in English from the College of St. Rose and a master's degree in pastoral counseling from Loyola College of Maryland. She has prepared media relations programs, spoken on media topics, and written for numerous publications including *America, Editor & Publisher, The Washington Post,* and *USA Today.* She also was producer of the award-winning video *Five Extraordinary Days* and has served as the editor of books that include the award-winning *John Paul II: A Light for the World* and *From John Paul II to Benedict XVI: An Inside Look at the End of an Era, the Beginning of a New One, and the Future of the Church.* She has been honored by several groups, including the New York State Bar Association, the New York Press Association, the Colorado Chapter of the Public Relations Society of America, the Catholic Press Association and the Catholic Academy for Communications Arts Professionals.

Father Thomas G. Weinandy, executive director of the USCCB's Secretariat of Doctrine, is a member of the Capuchin order. He holds a bachelor of arts degree in philosophy from St. Fidelis College in Herman, Pa.; a master's degree in systematic theology from Washington Theological

Union; and a doctorate in historical theology from King's College, University of London. Father Weinandy is a member of the Catholic Theological Society of America, the Fellowship of Catholic Scholars, The Academy of Catholic Theology, the North American Patristics Society, and the Association Internationale D'Etudes Patristiques. He is the author of fourteen books, including *Does God Change: The Word's Becoming in the Incarnation; Does God Suffer? Jesus the Christ; The Father's Spirit of Sonship: Reconceiving the Trinity; Athanasius: A Theological Introduction;* and *Sacrament of Mercy: A Spiritual and Practical Guide to Confession.* Father Weinandy has also published scholarly articles in such journals as *The Thomist, New Blackfriars, Communio, A Journal of Catholic Thought and Culture,* and the *International Journal of Systematic Theology.*

Cindy Wooden has been a correspondent in Catholic News Service's Rome Bureau since 1989. A graduate of Seattle University, she currently studies at the Institute for Interdisciplinary Studies on Religions and Culture at the Pontifical Gregorian University.

Ambassador Johnny Young, executive director of the USCCB's Office of Migration and Refugee Services, holds a bachelor of science degree, cum laude, from Temple University. He was a four-time American ambassador and holds the rank of career ambassador. His Foreign Service duty included service in eleven countries: five in Africa, three in the Middle East, two in Europe, and one in the Caribbean.

IN GRATITUDE

This tribute to Pope Benedict XVI has involved the efforts of many. Special thanks go to the bishops and staff of the United States Conference of Catholic Bishops, especially the U.S. bishops' Committee on Communications and the Catholic Communication Campaign, which provided funds to underwrite this effort.

Many USCCB staff extended themselves in a particular way. Among them were Helen Osman, secretary for communications, who expressed confidence in the project from its earliest days; staff of the USCCB Office for Media Relations, especially assistant directors Don Clemmer and Mar Muñoz-Visoso, administrative assistant Alverta Newton, and intern Margaret Aurand. Despite many other pressing obligations, they gave generously to this project.

USCCB Publishing contributed enthusiastically, especially designer Elisha Ann Busbee, editor Jeanette Fast Redmond, and researcher Elizabeth Cunningham. They worked assiduously with Paul Henderson, head of Publishing, and David Felber, associate director, who oversaw the entire production effort. Catholic News Service, the Washington-based news and photo service, also offered both assistance and photos from its archives. Special thanks also must be given to Father James Massa, director of the USCCB Secretariat of Ecumenical and Interreligious Affairs, who both wrote insightful essays and extended himself in reaching out to the Jewish and Islamic communities so wonderfully represented in this work, which shows the international significance of Pope Benedict.

Assistance also came from Rome, especially from Marjorie Weeke, who coordinated efforts at the Vatican—this book could not have come to fruition without her—and from the photo services of *L'Osservatore Romano* and the Catholic Press Photo, whose wonderful work makes this book the splendid tribute to Pope Benedict XVI that it is.

The many contributors whose names appear with their essays also deserve gratitude for their insightful contributions.

On a personal level, I must also thank the Sisters of Mercy of the Americas, my religious community, who offer unstinting support to my efforts for the Church and take special pride in this effort for our Holy Father.

When one lists names of people who deserve thanks, one does so at peril of overlooking some people, of course. If this has happened here, it is regretfully so.

Sister Mary Ann Walsh, RSM
Editor

INDEX

Index of General Subjects

Abdullah II of Jordan, 11, 201

ad limina visitations, 40, 200

Africa, Church in, 77-78, 205, 206, 208, 210, 211

Altötting, Our Lady of, 107, 203

Anglicans, 36, 206, 207, 211

anti-Semitism, 28, 63-66, 207, 208

Aparecida, Brazil, 80, 107

Augustine of Hippo (saint), 24, 108, 109, 198

Australia, 16, 18, 83, 177, 178, 207

Bartholomew I (patriarch of Constantinople), 36, 201, 206, 207

beatifications and canonizations, 200, 202, 205, 206

Benedict of Nursia (saint), 145, 146, 200, 208

Benedict XV, 18, 200

Benedict XVI, life and ministry of, 198-210. *See also* specific aspects

biomedical ethics, 31, 158, 168-69, 201

Black Madonna, 107

Blue Mosque, Istanbul, 18, 27, 54, 58-60

Brazil, 80, 107, 204, 207

Buddhism, 53, 200

Bush, George, 29, 190, 204

Cagrici, Mustafa, 54

camauro ("Santa hat"), 113

Cameroon, 77, 78, 208

canonizations and beatifications, 200, 202, 205, 206

Castel Gandolfo, 53, 120, 201, 209

The Catholic Channel, 95

Catholic education, 193

cats, 137-38

charity/love, 21, 24, 100, 127, 128, 138, 156, 161-63, 164, 212

Chico the cat, 137-38

children, 18, 23, 84, 127, 174, 187, 193

China, 32, 48-50, 204

clergy sexual abuse crisis, 18, 28, 72, 86, 150-52, 153, 207, 208, 211

coat of arms, papal, 108-9

Cologne, Germany, 31, 63, 83, 127, 132, 201

Congo, Democratic Republic of, 77

Congregation for the Doctrine of the Faith, 33, 199

"Cooperatores veritatis," 109, 198

✠ Cordero Lanza di Montezemolo, Andrea, 108, 109

Czech Republic, 44, 209

Czestochowa, Poland, 107

Darfur, 77

Democratic Republic of the Congo, 77

Dome of the Rock, Jerusalem, 60

Dunwoodie Seminary, New York, 84

economic ethics, 156-58, 161-63

ecumenism/unity, 21, 36-38, 48-50, 201, 202, 203, 204, 205, 206, 211

education, 44, 167, 187, 193

election of Benedict XVI, 15, 21, 23, 141, 168, 200

encyclicals. *See* Index of Sources

environmental concerns, 21, 24, 29, 158, 161, 177-78, 206, 209

ethics, 21, 23, 31, 156-58, 161-63, 168-69, 212

Eucharist, 31, 32, 100, 127, 128

Europe, Christian heritage of, 43-44

Facebook, 184

faith, 128

family life, 44, 142, 171, 174-75, 187

Fatima, 206, 211

foreign travels of Benedict XVI, 16, 18, 23-24, 28, 36, 58-60, 63, 70-72, 84, 171-72, 201-9, 211. *See also* specific places

Ganswein, Georg, 138

Genoa, Italy, 142

Germany, 16, 27, 31, 36, 43, 47, 58, 63, 70, 107, 108, 127, 132, 137, 146, 150, 171, 177, 201, 203, 211

globalization, 174

green technology, 21, 24, 29, 158, 161, 177-78, 206, 209

Ground Zero (World Trade Center site), New York City, 16

Hinduism, 53

Holocaust, 28, 63-66, 202, 207, 208, 213

Holy Land. *See* Israel; Jordan; Palestinian Territories

Holy Sepulchre, Jerusalem, 124

hope, 21, 83, 127, 128, 168, 194, 212

human rights, 167

India, 31

interfaith dialogue. *See* specific faiths, e.g. Judaism

Internet presence, 28, 184-85, 208
Iraq, 172, 201, 202, 204, 205, 206, 207
Ireland, 150-52, 204, 208, 211
Islam, 11, 16, 18, 27, 53-54, 58-60, 200, 203, 205, 206, 207, 209
Israel, 12, 16, 18, 60, 124, 171, 201, 203, 204, 208
Israeli-Palestinian conflict, 171, 190, 203
Istanbul, Turkey, 18, 27, 36
Jainism, 53
Jerusalem, 18, 60, 124
John XXIII, 43, 113, 213
John Paul II, 31, 70, 80, 83, 104, 113, 123, 198, 200
Jordan, 11, 16, 58, 201, 208
Judaism, 12, 18, 28, 53, 63-66, 201, 205, 206, 207, 208, 211, 213
justice, 77, 161-63, 164, 167
Küng, Hans, 53, 201
Latin American bishops, 80, 200, 204, 207
Lefebvre, Marcel, 21, 201, 213
Leo XIII, 163
liturgy, 31, 66, 127-28, 132, 134-35, 204, 213
Lourdes, 107, 205, 207
love/charity, 21, 24, 100, 127, 128, 138, 156, 161-63, 164, 212
Lutheran World Federation, 36-38
Malta, 16, 18, 211
Marian devotion, 107, 123, 205
Marktl Am Inn, Germany, 47, 107, 198
marriage, 44, 187, 201
Meisner, Joachim, 120
migrants and refugees, 174-75
Mozart, 48, 119-20
music, 48, 119-20
Muslims. *See* Islam
National Shrine of the Immaculate Conception, Washington, D.C., 107
Nationals Park, Washington D.C., 16
Nazism, 28, 32, 63, 171, 198, 202, 207
New York City, 16, 24, 95, 142
Obama, Barack, 18, 29-31, 190, 209
Orthodox Christianity, 36, 201, 202, 203, 204, 205, 206, 209, 211
L'Osservatore Romano, 108, 120, 203
Pakistan, 31
Palestinian-Israeli conflict, 171, 190, 203
Palestinian Territories, 16, 171, 202, 204, 208, 210
pallium, 108, 113-14, 132
Park East Synagogue, New York City, 63

pastor, Benedict XVI as, 16-21, 40, 159
Paul (saint and apostle), 31, 127, 207
Paul VI, 80, 107, 113, 156, 199, 212
peace, 18, 21, 53, 77, 163, 167, 171-72, 187
peace, sign of, 128
Pelosi, Nancy, 208
Peres, Shimon, 12, 204
Petrillo, Saverio, 120
piano playing of Benedict XVI, 119-20
Pius V, 213
Pius XI, 202
Pius XII, 206
Poland, 47, 107, 146, 202, 203
political life, 18, 77, 158, 161, 164, 174, 188-90, 201
poverty and the poor, 77, 80, 158, 161, 164, 207, 210, 211
prayer and contemplation, 31, 142, 146
priestly life and ministry, 142, 146, 208, 209
Rahner, Karl, 123
Ratzinger, Georg, 119, 120, 198
Ratzinger, Joseph, 15, 33, 40, 43-44, 103, 108, 113, 117, 123, 137, 168, 171, 182, 198-99
red shoes, 113
refugees and migrants, 174-75
Regensburg, Germany, 27, 58, 60, 203
religious freedom, 31-32, 48-50, 167, 202, 204
religious life, 142, 145
right to life, 21, 29-31, 158, 167, 168-69, 187, 201, 205, 208
rights, human, 167
Rome, Great Synagogue of, 12, 211
saints, creating, 200, 202, 205, 206
"Santa hat" (camauro), 113
Savona, Italy, 142
Schneier, Arthur, 63
Second Vatican Council, 38, 43, 63, 113, 123, 127, 134, 174, 198, 202, 213
sexual exploitation: clergy sexual abuse crisis, 18, 28, 72, 86, 150-52, 153, 207, 208, 211; of migrants and refugees, 174
sign of peace, 128
Sistine Chapel, 21, 36, 119, 141, 149, 211
social networking, 184-85
social teachings of Church, 161-63, 164, 167
Society of St. Pius X, 28, 36, 201, 208, 210, 213
Somalia, 77
Spain, 187, 203, 211

221

St. Patrick's Cathedral, New York City, 16, 24, 95

St. Peter's Square, 32, 55, 123, 204, 205, 206

Sudan, 77

Sydney, Australia, 83, 177, 178, 207

Synod of Bishops: on Africa, 77-78, 210; on the Eucharist, 127, 134, 201, 202, 212; on the Middle East, 209; on the Word of God, 31, 123, 207

teacher, Benedict XVI as, 103, 123, 134

theology, Joseph Ratzinger as professor of, 53, 113, 123, 193, 198

Tridentine Mass, 31, 128, 204, 213

truth, 23, 44, 53, 100, 109, 156, 163

Turkey, 16, 18, 27, 36, 205

United Nations, 23, 31, 70, 77, 167, 172, 190, 204, 207, 210, 211

United States, papal visits to, 16, 18, 24, 28-31, 70-72, 84, 86-88, 90, 95, 107, 132, 142, 145, 150, 172, 193

unity/ecumenism, 21, 36-38, 48-50, 201, 202, 203, 204, 205, 206, 211

Universal Declaration of Human Rights, 167

Valencia, Spain, 187, 203

Vatican II, 38, 43, 63, 113, 123, 127, 134, 174, 198, 202, 213

Vietnam, 203

vocations, 142, 145, 146

Washington, D.C., 16, 28, 72, 84, 86, 107, 150

Western Wall, Jerusalem, 18

White House, 8, 16, 172, 188-90

Williams, Rowan, 36, 207, 211

Williamson, Richard, 28, 36, 208, 213

women, 174

World Day of Communications, 184-85

World Day of Consecrated Life, 145

World Day of Migrants and Refugees, 174, 175

World Day of Peace, 167, 171, 187

World Day of Prayer for Vocations, 142

World Meeting of Families, 187

World Trade Center site, New York City, 16

World Youth Day, 16, 31, 32, 62, 70, 83, 127, 132, 177, 178, 201, 207

Yad Vashem, 66

Yankee Stadium, New York City, 16, 142

Yaoundé, Cameroon, 77

Year of Africa, 77-78

Year for Priests, 31, 146, 149, 209

Year of St. Paul, 31, 207

young people, 83, 84, 127, 142

YouTube, 184-85, 208

✠ Index of Sources

Address at the White House, Washington (April 16, 2008), 8

Address to Cardinals (April 20, 2005), 24

Anglicanorum Coetibus (November 9, 2009), 211

Caritas in Veritate (*Charity in Truth*) (June 29, 2009), 21, 23, 100, 156-58, 161-63, 164, 168, 172, 177, 187, 209, 212

Certain Aspects of the Doctrine on the Church (July 10, 2007), 204

The Church in Africa in Service to Reconciliation, Justice and Peace (October 2009), 77, 78

A Common Word Between Us and You (October 13, 2007), 58, 205

Deus Caritas Est (*God Is Love*) (December 25, 2005), 21, 24, 100, 128, 138, 156, 161, 164, 188, 202, 212

Dignitas Personae (*The Dignity of a Person*) (December 12, 2008), 31

Jesus of Nazareth (Benedict XVI), 24, 66, 204, 213

Joseph and Chico: The Life of Pope Benedict XVI as Told by a Cat (Jeanne Perego), 137-38

Letter at the beginning of the Year for Priests (June 18, 2009), 149

Letter to Bishops on the Lifting of the Excommunication of Lefebvrite Bishops (March 10, 2009), 208, 213

Letter to Chinese Catholics (May 27, 2007), 48-50, 213

Milestones: Memoirs 1927-1977 (Joseph Ratzinger), 177

Regensburg speech, 2006, 27, 58, 60

Sacramentum Caritatis (*The Sacrament of Charity*) (February 22, 2007), 127, 135, 203, 212

Spe Salvi (*On Christian Hope*) (November 30, 2007), 21, 127, 194, 205, 212

The Spirit of the Liturgy (Joseph Ratzinger), 127

Summorum Pontificum (July 7, 2007), 128, 204, 212-13

Urbi et Orbi messages
April 19, 2005, 104
Easter 2009, 114

Yad Vashem Holocaust Memorial speech (May 11, 2009), 66

Index of Photos

Abdullah II of Jordan and family, 10

Aboriginal dancers, 74-75

Altötting, Our Lady of, 106

Andrews Air Force Base, 72

Angola, 78

Aosta, Italy, 20-21, 110-11, 118-19, 141, 180-81

Auschwitz concentration camp, 42-43

Australia, 74-75, 130-31

Baka tribe, Cameroon, 76

Bartholomew I (patriarch of Constantinople), 38-39, 56-57

Baxendale, Janet, 144

Benedict XVI. *See* specific locations, events, and accompanying persons

Bethlehem, Caritas Baby Hospital, 169

birthday celebration at White House, 89

Blue Mosque, Istanbul, Turkey, 59, 60, 61

Brazil, 81

broken wrist, Benedict XVI with, 141

Buddhist leader Dr. Jongmae Kenneth Park, 41

Bush, George and Laura, 86-87

Cagrici, Mustafa (grand mufti of Istanbul), 59, 61

camauro ("Santa hat"), 112

Cameroon, 46, 76, 78-79

Caritas Baby Hospital, Bethlehem, 169

Caritas in Veritate, signing of, 157, 158

Castel Gandolfo, 50, 104-5, 123, 140

cellphones, crowds taking pictures with, 186

children, 14, 33, 46, 76, 78-79, 81, 85, 97, 101, 110-11, 159, 169, 186, 192

clergy sexual abuse, survivor of, 152

coat of arms in topiary, Palazzo del Governatorato, Vatican City, 109

Cohen, Shear-Yashuv Cohen (chief rabbi of Haifa), 67

Cologne, Germany, 2-3, 102

confetti at youth meeting in Genoa, Italy, 133

disabilities, children with, 85, 159

Dome of the Rock, Jerusalem, 26-27, 54

Fazenda da Esperança (Farm of Hope), Guaratinguetá, Brazil, 81

fourth anniversary of election of Benedict XVI, 49

Genoa, Italy, confetti at youth meeting in, 133

Germany, 2-3, 102, 106

Ground Zero (World Trade Center site), New York City, 91

Guaratinguetá, Brazil, 81

✠ Hall of Remembrance, Yad Vashem Holocaust memorial, Jerusalem, 62, 68-69

hats worn by Benedict XVI, 112, 114

Holy Sepulchre, Jerusalem, 4-5

Hussain, Saman, 52-53

Israel, 13, 169. *See also* Jerusalem

Istanbul, Turkey, 38-39, 56-57, 59, 60, 61

Italy: Aosta, 20-21, 110-11, 118-19, 141; Castel Gandolfo, 50, 104-5, 123, 140; Genoa, confetti at youth meeting in, 133; Lorenzago di Cadore, 176, 178-79; Onna, L'Aquila, tent camp at, 195. *See also* Vatican

Jerusalem: Dome of the Rock, 26-27, 54; Hall of Remembrance, Yad Vashem Holocaust memorial, 62, 68-69; Holy Sepulchre, 4-5; streets of walled city, 25; welcome banners in, 172-73; Western Wall, 64-65

Jewish leaders, Benedict XVI with, 13, 40, 62, 67, 68-69

John Paul II: with Benedict XVI, 148; fourth anniversary Mass for death of, 132; staff of, 165

Jordan: Abdullah II of Jordan and family, 10; Amman, presentation of eucharistic gifts at Mass in, 135; Mount Nebo, 30; Regina Pacis (Queen of Peace) Center, 183

kaffiyeh, Benedict XVI in, 183

King, Bernice, 37

Korean Buddhist Taego Order leader Dr. Jongmae Kenneth Park, 41

Les Combes, Valle d'Aosta, Italy, 20-21, 110-11, 118-19, 141

lion cub from Medrano Circus, 136-37

Lorenzago di Cadore, Italy, 176, 178-79

Maison of St. Bernard, Martigny, Swiss Alps, 138-39

Medrano Circus lion cub, 136-37

Missionaries of Charity, 95

Mount Nebo, Jordan, 30

music, 49, 68-69, 118-19, 121

Muslim leaders, Benedict XVI with, 26-27, 52-53, 54, 59, 60, 61

National Shrine of the Immaculate Conception, Washington, D.C., 16-17, 106, 125, 126

Nationals Park, Washington, D.C., 33, 88, 90, 115, 151, 196

New York City: JFK International Airport departure ceremony, 170-71; Park East Synagogue, 40; St. Joseph's Seminary, Yonkers, New York, 45, 82, 85, 96, 143,

159, 192; St. Patrick's Cathedral, 94, 95, 128-29, 144; UN assembly, Benedict XVI at, 47, 160-61, 166; World Trade Center site, 91; Yankee Stadium, 29, 72-73, 92-93, 116, 147, 175

nun, Benedict XVI giving communion to, 95

Obama, Barack and Michelle, 190-91

Onna, L'Aquila, Italy, tent camp at, 195

Orthodox patriarch Bartholomew I, 38-39, 56-57

L'Osservatore Romano, Benedict XVI reading, 162-63

Palazzo del Governatorato, Vatican City, coat of arms in topiary, 109

Park, Dr. Jongmae Kenneth, 41

Park East Synagogue, New York City, 40

Peres, Shimon, 13

Pilarczyk, Daniel, 16-17

Pope John Paul II Cultural Center, Washington, D.C., 41, 52-53

Ratzinger, Georg (brother of Benedict XVI), 121

Regina Pacis (Queen of Peace) Center, Amman, Jordan, 183

"Santa hat" (camauro), 112

Saturno hat, 114

Sistine Chapel, 121

soldier, Benedict XVI giving communion to, 88

St. Bernard dogs with Benedict XVI, Swiss Alps, 138-39

St. Joseph's Seminary, Yonkers, New York, 45, 82, 85, 96, 143, 159, 192

St. Patrick's Cathedral, New York City, 94, 95, 128-29, 144

St. Peter's Basilica, Rome, 6, 9, 154, 165, 182

St. Peter's Square, Rome, 32, 55, 98, 117, 182

Swiss Alps, Maison of St. Bernard, Martigny, 138-39

Sydney, Australia, 74-75, 130-31

Tel Aviv, Shimon Peres with Benedict XVI in, 13

tent camp, Onna, L'Aquila, Italy, 195

Thavis, John, 71

Turkey, 38-39, 56-57, 59, 60, 61

United Nations, 47, 160-61, 166

United States: bishops, 16-17, 94, 125; Bush, George and Laura, 86-87; children waiting to greet Pope in, 97; King, Bernice, with Benedict XVI, 37; Obama, Barack and Michelle, 190-91; reporters on plane flight to U.S., 70-71. *See also* New York City; Washington, D.C.

Valle d'Aosta, Italy, 20-21, 110-11, 118-19, 141

Vatican: aerial view of Vatican City, 22; balcony in papal residence, Benedict XVI on, 34; Caritas in Veritate, signing of, 157, 158; Cohen, Shear-Yashuv (chief rabbi of Haifa), with Benedict XVI, 67; gardens, Benedict XVI strolling in, 124; Medrano Circus lion cub, Benedict XVI with, 136-37; Obama, Barack and Michelle, 190-91; papal coat of arms in topiary, Palazzo del Governatorato, 109; papal office, Benedict XVI on telephone in, 210; Sistine Chapel, 121; St. Peter's Basilica, 6, 9, 154, 165, 182; St. Peter's Square, 32, 55, 98, 117, 182; Synod Hall, with cardinals, 19; Web site, 185

Vatican Diplomatic Corps, 50-51

Washington, D.C.: Andrews Air Force Base, 72; National Shrine of the Immaculate Conception, 16-17, 106, 125, 126; Nationals Park, 33, 88, 90, 115, 151, 196; Pope John Paul II Cultural Center, 41, 52-53; White House, 86-87, 89, 188-89

Western Wall, Jerusalem, 64-65

White House, 86-87, 89, 188-89

World Trade Center site, New York City, 91

World Youth Day: Cologne, Germany, 44, 102; Sydney, Australia, 74-75, 130-31

Yad Vashem Holocaust memorial, Israel, 62, 68-69

Yankee Stadium, New York City, 29, 72-73, 92-93, 116, 147, 175

Yaoundé, Cameroon, 46

young people, 45, 68-69, 78-79, 82, 96, 102, 192